Learning About Dogs

Teaching with
Reinforcement

**FOR EVERY DAY AND
IN EVERY WAY**

Kay Laurence

Printed in the U.S. and distributed by
Karen Pryor ClickerTraining and Sunshine Books
49 River Street, Waltham, MA 02453
www.clickertraining.com
Sales: U.S. Toll Free 1-800-472-5425
        781-398-0754

First published in 2009 by
Learning About Dogs Limited
PO Box 13, Chipping Campden, Glos, GL55 6WX. UK

ISBN 978-1-890948-40-5

Books by Kay Laurence:

Clicker Training: The Perfect Foundation, and DVD
Clicker Intermediate Trainer Level 3, and DVD
Clicker World Competition Obedience
Clicker Dances with Dogs
Learning Games

DVDs by Kay Laurence:

Teaching Self Control: Whippits Training
Teaching Flexigility: Cavaletti

available from:

www.clickertraining.com

Cover picture: Six week old collie pups, with an exclusive
reinforcement history of sitting for life's rewards. photo by H. Zulch.

CONTENTS

1 Understanding Reinforcement

Many of us enjoy teaching in a positive style. It demands us to be more creative than the alternatives, and certainly it can force us to take the long route rather than the easier short cuts. But the benefits of this style of teaching is a really happy learner, who develops with a keen interest in acquiring new skills and we also get a buzz out of knowing we have caused no harm, just sealed our relationship.

At Wagmore Barn I teach many varied classes. From experienced clicker trainers interested in specialised activities to people making their first contact with positive teaching in the puppy and junior classes. I am also fortunate to teach in many places outside the UK and view hundreds of different styles of clicker training, not just my home grown learners.

Many of us succeed in teaching complex skills with talented and sometimes less talented dogs, and often helping a partnership find a happier, balanced life. But there are some people who find that although they follow the prescribed protocols, the results are below their expectations. Their dog is given lots of attention for a sit when greeting, but still jumps up.

There are some dogs that find it hard to learn new behaviours with consistency. They learn a great heelwork style but seem to droop with predictability despite lots of clicks and treats when in the correct position.

On the surface everything seems to be on track but when exploring a little deeper there are undercurrents affecting the behaviour: reinforcement patterns.

I have grown more respectful of these powerful currents over the recent years. We have examined many ways of teaching and communicating to dogs and learners, and have developed an extensive library of skills and tools to teach high quality behaviours with ease. We can become addicted to this learning acquisition period which brings us a great sense of achievement, and clicker training with a high rate treat delivery can ease us into a feeling of having completed the job. Now we need to explore further and really examine all the subtle elements that distort behaviours.

I am often found reminding people that it is the nature of behaviour to change. But what is changing the behaviour? The reinforcers. I have a young collie pup at present who is developing an eye for herding his relatives. Every single time he gets to use this skill the behaviour changes. It is a self reinforcing activity that exponentially magnifies in pleasure each time he uses it. At present this is on track. But what if he diverted his "eye" to herding traffic instead of his relatives? Every single time the pup was exposed to traffic and allowed to use the behaviour it would become more reinforced, stronger and much harder to reduce or eliminate. The reinforcement history of the behaviour would dictate how we plan to change the behaviour. Every week it would take a different strategy to manage the behaviour since the reinforcement is changing.

TREATS AND REWARDS

One of our failings is the habit of saying one thing but having a different intent. We may reward or treat our dog with the delivery of food but are somewhat disappointed in the result. We sigh as we give the treat. It "taints" the reward. We tell them they are a good dog, but look away as we secretly wish they were better. We get wrapped up in our own intent, and can be lazy in actually analysing what is happening and what is needed.

We wear a feeling of satisfaction that we have rewarded the good sit and never allowed the jumping up to gain our attention, but the jumping up still occurs. It doesn't matter what we think we have rewarded—that is our own selfish assessment—what has been reinforced is the jumping up.

If the behaviour repeats, gets stronger or happens more frequently then it is being reinforced. It absolutely doesn't matter what you think you are rewarding, the behaviour is being reinforced. Your intention is of no value, intentions cannot act as reinforcers.

> **reward** *n.*1. something given in return for a deed or service rendered. 2. a sum of money offered, esp. for help in finding a criminal or missing property. 3. something received in return for good or evil; deserts. *~vb.* 4. to give something to (someone) esp. in gratitude for a service rendered.

> reinforce *vb*. 1. to give added strength or support to. 2. to give
> added emphasis to; increase; "his rudeness reinforced my deter-
> mination". 3. to give added support to (a military force) by
> providing more men or equipment

Reward implies an interaction, an exchange of something done for someone else, the person rewarding gains something from the actions of the person, dog being rewarded.

A reinforcer does not imply a pay back for the deliverer of the reinforcer. It has a more independent association, where the action is being reinforced, and is not giving back to the reinforcer.

Once we begin to see the reinforcer "currents" that surround us all the time we can begin to become more effective and more efficient in our teaching and interaction.

THE SCIENCE

<u>A reinforcer</u> is that which makes a behaviour stronger, happen more frequently and resistant to extinguishing.

<u>A punisher</u> is the opposite: that which makes a behaviour weaker, happen less frequently, fade or completely extinguish.

These terms "rewards" and "punishers" have led us into trouble. We have a dislike of using the term "punishment" because of the association of aversive punishment—that which causes the dog pain or harm. Punishment alone diminishes behaviour. By just ignoring an attempt for attention we can punish the behaviour, perhaps we were too busy to notice, but we delivered punishment.

It was not our intention to cause harm or discomfort, but the behaviour would become less likely to repeat. Our intentions get us into all sorts of problems, especially when we use terminology inaccurately.

To become more effective in our shaping of behaviour we have to learn to remove our emotional needs woven into the communication. We love to feel we are avoiding punishment and rewarding our dogs, when in truth we should be reinforcing behaviours. By operating in that layer above our emotional involvement we triple our effectiveness and make it far easier for our dogs to learn. They just want to get it right, they know they are important but please give me clear information!

Effective punishment should only diminish the behaviour, not the dog or the relationship. The dangerous zone, that causes the disappointing results, is unintentional punishment and reinforcement delivered to the wrong behaviour. By improving our ability to see what is happening, measure the outcomes without emotional analysis, and deliver the reinforcer accurately we can see immediate improvements and move closer to our goals.

"The real voyage of discovery consists not in seeking new landscapes, but in seeing with new eyes."

— Marcel Proust

2 Types of Reinforcers

Behaviour is in a constant state of change. In fact the one thing you can guarantee is that it is the nature of behaviour to change. You may believe that you will always love chocolate, that it is a fixed behaviour and it does not change. But if you have eaten so much that the idea of another piece makes you feel uncomfortable, then your behaviour has changed. Working for two weeks in a chocolate factory served to associate severe displeasure with the smell of cooking chocolate for me. What was a reinforcer stopped being a reinforcer and slipped over to the dark side—a punisher. This can be temporary or permanent depending on how traumatic the punishment is.

If behaviour is constantly shifting then the reinforcers and their values are shifting as well. The reinforcer is entirely defined by the effect it has on the behaviour. If the dog is tired, another chase after a ball could be one chase too many, if the dog is full another piece of food may be taken by habit, but make the dog feel more uncomfortable. And at that moment, being allowed to rest becomes the most high value reinforcer.

We have many, many different types of reinforcers available and success in using them depends on our skill of being able to apply them appropriately and effectively. Choosing the right reinforcer that maintains or strengthens the behaviour at that time, in the right quantity, is critical.

Reinforcers can generally be split into two categories: natural reinforcers (primary reinforcers) that need no previous experience to be reinforcing; such as food, security, using instinctive behaviours, and learned or associated reinforcers (secondary reinforcers); such as a clicker, a "good boy", retrieving a ball. (Chasing the ball is a primary reinforcer, using an instinctive behaviour, but retrieving the ball to a person to elicit another throw would be learned from experience).

I want to examine each reinforcer and the effect it has on behaviour. None are perfect or suit every situation, behaviour or receiver. Reinforcers also have greatly different values and in one situation a slice of meat will be a reinforcer but not when a more valued reinforcer is possible. My Gordons are reinforced by the bird hunting process and food is of no value in that situation, similarly with the collies when herding. Away from that environment food is very high value.

PRIMARY REINFORCERS

FOOD

This is considered a primary reinforcer, that reinforces without prior knowledge or understanding. In normal circumstances it is probably considered the easiest to use, but the misuse opens many problems.

I feed my dogs raw food and soon discovered that sticking to these principles when delivering a reinforcer became highly ineffective. Raw meat sticks to the fingers like glue, and if dropped to the floor attracts every atom of dust and fluff in the vicinity. It cannot be stored in a pocket, it is not easy to deliver with speed, and it is difficult to divide into tiny portions. These may be obstacles that can be circumvented, but a good example of my dogs' main diet not being suitable as a reinforcer in training.

Raw food is very high on the primary reinforcer list as baby puppies of 3 weeks recognise the smell of warm, raw meat and eat with only a second's hesitation. The scent awakens a recognition that this is needed, it is not a learned response, it is an instinctive response. In the past when the dog breeders fell in love with specially prepared commercial food you needed to teach a puppy to eat soaked kibble. Go far enough back and relate to the natural process of the pups eating regurgitated raw meat and we have a primary reinforcer.

For the first 7–10 days I feed my pups their warm, wet, raw meat from my fingers. If it is slightly wet it doesn't stick, and since it has been kept in the fridge I bring it up to "stomach" temperature with a 10 minute soak in warm water. I haven't quite regressed enough to chew it and spit it out, the simulation of warm, wet and raw works sufficiently well. At the same time the pups are eating from my hands, they are associating human scent with a reinforcer. Licking my fingers is a noticeable reinforcer for my dogs, and they never fail to recognise my scent. My scent becomes a secondary reinforcer.

Food and the process of eating can carry an enormous amount of baggage. Every now and then a pup or adult dog comes along that does not seem find food a high value reinforcer. Sometimes this can be traced back to illness as a youngster, but very often it is over zealous caring of the puppies where they have been over fed, or fed on demand so that the relief of hunger is not learned through eating. Good quality food cannot be replaced by great quantity. It is normal for pups to be competitive when eating. This begins within minutes of being born where the pup has to fight to find the teats and their first milk. Siblings will jostle and push against each other for a teat which encourages an arousing competition to find a teat and then grip on for dear life. Litters with very low numbers, or even singles may not develop this competitive desire to eat.

From the nutritional aspect the breeder wants to ensure that all pups get an equal chance to eat without the smallest pup losing out. There are some excellent systems that provide each pup with their own bowl replacing the free for all that was the norm. But step back a little further and we realise that bowl feeding is a modern invention, and pups would normally share a carcass, or break off a portion to take away and eat alone. Ideally some degree of competitive and co-operative eating would be normal, and complete inhibition of this may lead to a "picky" eater.

Usually fussy eaters are taught to be fussy. Like many unwanted behaviours a simple single event leads to a lifetime of baggage. On offering the pup the usual dinner, which was refused, more enticing food was substituted and the pup made a connection between the behaviour of refusing and the extra attention or more appetising food that was offered. Pups can refuse, they can have sore gums or have just tried to digest the Sunday Times newspaper or simply be too tired. Never mind, once is not a problem, a series of successive refusals is a symptom of something out of balance.

Stress will also inhibit eating. It is a survival mechanism to keep our resources focussed on fight or flight responses. Full tummies would reduce our ability to do either. Nature withdraws the digestive resources to route to other more important areas. Ever experienced a dry mouth when you are nervous? Try eating a full meal when you are over excited. It is simply the wrong thing to do.

To eat, and enjoy eating, you need to be relaxed and have a sense of security. In fact your digestive process is probably more efficient when in that state. In class we use the natural eating inhibition to measure the mental state of a dog or pup. Pups, or even adult dogs, can be overwhelmed by the class environment and naturally refuse food. This stress level greatly diminishes learning, so trying to train would be ineffective. When offered food is taken the pup is more relaxed, threats have been assessed, they have a sense of security with their owner's contact and learning can begin. Pups come to class, remain seated on laps or in contact with the owners and are regularly assessed through the class. When they begin to eat we consider they have "enrolled".

It would be easy to understand that if the assessment process was disregarded and the dog or pup forced to "train" or move around the class, "socialising", their level of stress and anxiety would be associated with the experience, and similar experiences would become highly unpleasant.

If you like to train with food remember that although it is a primary, natural reinforcer a refusal of food should be noted. It may be an indication of stress or that the dog has come to expect a higher value reinforcer in connection with that behaviour.

TYPES OF FOOD

Small treats are frequently used to reinforce behaviours, especially when building new behaviours. We need certain practical considerations for this task to be effective:

TASTY, EASILY DIGESTED

Wet food is usually more appetising than dry food. Kibble and pre-packaged treats can be easily kept in the pocket for random reinforcement, but frequent feeding over a 10 minute session can leave the dog with a dry mouth and an essential need to drink lots of water over the next hour. Dry food was not designed to be fed in any quantity dry, it is a convenience for packaging and weight. Imagine eating an entire packet of biscuits without a cup of tea?

Raw food has certain practical problems, but small pieces of cooked meats, or specially cooked "cake" (which is often more fudge-like cubes of baked meat, liver, eggs and flour), jerky, sandwich meats are ideal. They are also easily managed in containers and handled without too much stickiness. But I have learned through experience to stop putting my fingers in my mouth or eating a sandwich without washing my hands. A liver flavoured doughnut was not reinforcing!

The scent of your food will also become a strong cue and motivator for the dog, as will your clothes. As the dog experiences more pleasure from the highly reinforcing training sessions, the smell of your food treats will trigger an excitement, anticipation and increased production of saliva. All contributing to the perfect fore runner of an interactive session. Your hands will also become focus points from their scent, this may or may not be an advantage, but we certainly use our hands in excess when communicating and this may easily help the dog. Equally your onboard treat bag or pocket will trigger attention. To prevent setting up predictable patterns take extra care to be flexible and vary the routines. If your dog discovers that you only reinforce when you are wearing your training outfit, they can learn that you are ineffective at all other times. Dogs can learn from a single event, especially when the outcome is highly reinforcing. Food is only one reinforcer and we need to have a complete menu of reinforcers available at all times.

SIZE

This is an important factor when using high rates of reinforcement. We need to be able to reinforce 20 times in one minute, over a 10 minutes of training that becomes 200 pieces of food. This high rate is exponentially more reinforcing than one pile of treats at the end of the session. The dogs make a strong connection between the behaviour and the reinforcers, and a high sense of achievement—a primary reinforcer. Commercially prepared treats or biscuits can often be designed for the dog to take away and enjoy at leisure or involve some chewing process to add to the pleasure. These are unsuitable for training purposes unless a time delay is desired. A pup settling down their crate is a perfect situation for a longer reinforcer.

Very small dogs and pups will fill too quickly for effective training unless their treats are the size of a piece of rice. You can even use the "lick" technique to reduce the portions again. There is cheese in a tube, also paté on your finger. I begin each session measuring a portion for that dog that is never larger than the dog's skull, i.e; their stomach size. Once that is finished, there is at least a 30 minute rest to empty the stomach before any further training. They may say they want more, but I want an empty tum! You must also reduce their regular meals by an equivalent portion, unless your training sessions are highly energetic and burning up the extra intake.

From practice and experience I find sliced sandwich meats are ideal. Chicken is probably the least offensive, it peels apart easily like flicking coins. Other meats such as liver roll, luncheon meat, sausage types and ham are also good. You can cook and slice your own sausages or frankfurters. Preserved meats often contain a lot of salt to improve the flavour and the dogs can get quite thirsty. We use chicken most of the time and sausages or cheese as reserves. Hard cheese can be chopped up into small half centimetre cubes. Cooked liver and heart is something extra special. You can use the highest desired food at times when focus is questionable. The more fat content the more appetising. One year we had to "recycle" a lamb that had got over fat at the wrong time of year, and the scrap fats were THE Best reinforcers I have ever used, for every dog in class. Such focus! Choosing the right quality reinforcer to match the behaviour in the sufficient amount to strengthen or maintain the behaviour is key skill covered later in Chapter 4.

MANAGING THE FOOD

Store the food in a variety of places, in particular the locations where you will need a quick supply. My dogs like to run around the garden last thing at night checking out the foxes and other night life. It can turn a bit rowdy and coming in to bed can be delayed. On that particular "call in" there are treats waiting in the kitchen, one of the larger, chewy commercial treats, and a reminder of this guarantees no loitering in the garden.

Always have some prepared ready to go from the fridge, and long-life supplies around the house. Learning is not restricted to specific sessions. You will want to be able to reward the dog, especially a pup, to establish lifeskills, many times through the day. All dogs, but especially youngsters, benefit from reinforcement for good behaviour as soon as it occurs.

Pocket mugging can become a problem—especially if you reinforce it. I could ask you why you reinforced it but it was probably one of those single event learning situations that occur when we undergo a single event lapse of focus.

I am guilty of searching for clothes with suitable food pockets, and have a range of fleece jackets with the pockets chewed out. But I do urge you to check all pockets before washing. Ham flavoured "clean" clothes are not well received in public.

YOUR REINFORCEMENT

This is a tricky area but food preparation and delivery is a highly reinforcing process for some people. It becomes synonymous with caring and demonstrating love for the recipient. At our classes we have professional foodies who regularly exchange liver fudge recipes and thoroughly enjoy the process of finding the very best reinforcers for their dog. At the other extreme are the folk who may remember to buy a tin of hot dogs from the local shop, but forget the can opener!

We also get mixed up between reinforcement and indulgence. I do not think you have to become so scientifically based that you can never, or would never, indulge, but if a dog performs a behaviour to a certain standard and gets a treat, but then repeats the behaviour at a lower standard and still gets the treat we are giving very mixed messages. We have reinforced a variable standard and can only expect variable results. Whilst out on a walk you call your dog and get a tremendously quick response. On arrival the dog gets the treat, the next time you call, the dog hesitates over the very interesting smell, takes the time to cock his leg, then strolls towards you and still gets a treat you have reinforced both behaviours. "Aaah ..... but he still came when I called him". But was it as treat worthy as the first recall? You will still reinforce but this time appropriate to the effort of the behaviour and you will need the self discipline to lower your reinforcer, and not take the easy route because of that single event loss of focus moment.

SUITABILITY

Food covers a good range of behaviours we may want to reinforce, with the exception of high activity. The dog may need to pant at quite a fast rate and swallowing may be compromised. On occasion when training heelwork with a high head carriage the food can go down to wrong way unless the dog lowers their head.

Food may not be suitable for dogs that become so over aroused at the prospect of a piece of food they are unable to maintain the behaviours. Although the higher the desire for the food the easier it is to generate and reinforce self control. These dogs would find learning relaxation with food an impossibility.

WHEN IT STOPS BEING A REINFORCER

Food has a limitation. The dog may begin to feel uncomfortable but not be able to stop eating. I notice this especially with clicker training, where the habit of eating after the click is so strong that the dog cannot refuse. The technique of pushing the food at the dog will also cover this state of fullness. Where as when tossing a piece of food you can observe the dog's eagerness to follow and eat. Some dogs will always have room for one more treat, but that doesn't mean it is good for them!

Stress can also inhibit appetite, the dry mouth is a symptom of high levels of stress, and a good indicator that digestion is likely to be compromised as well. A pile of treats sitting heavily in the stomach does not make too good a reinforcer.

If the dog is hesitant to eat, do not persuade or encourage. Take it as communication, and at this time, that piece of food will not be a reinforcer.

USING AN INSTINCTIVE BEHAVIOUR

Over many years of experience in teaching many different types of dogs, and sharing my life with two breeds with strongly defined instincts, I am left with no doubt that using the inherited instinct is reinforcing. The more the behaviour is used, the more it becomes reinforced.

Baby puppies are born with an instinct to leave the nest to urinate at about 10–14 days. This depends on their walking skills, and the opportunity to find the edge of the nest. They will hardly see where they are going, but make every effort to move away from the centre of the sleeping area. By four weeks, with only two weeks of practice, this will have become a strong behaviour. Pups move off the bed on waking, all peeing in unison, and make every attempt to take a poo as far away as possible from the bed. What begins as an instinctive urge, is allowed to be reinforced through use, and naturally develops into a strong behaviour. If the initial development is inhibited, often through the entire bedding and play area being of the same surface, the instinct can be inhibited and almost lost and to replace the behaviour it needs to be taught, with external reinforcement for emptying in the chosen area. This is an instinctive behaviour common to all dogs, which has been enhanced to define the "nest" as our house or even garden area, and the dogs able to maintain control until in an appropriate environment. It began at 2 weeks of age.

There is a massive list of common behaviours that given the chance to emerge turn into strong life long behaviours.

THE DESIRE TO LEARN

This emerges in the pups from 3 weeks of age, where they explore, taste, sniff, and touch as many new things as possible. Their environment is examined, they enjoy activities with their siblings, they bite every part of every sibling discovering what responses occur. In turn the siblings learn to avoid uncomfortable biting and over 4 weeks of playing they develop a protocol for playing. They have learned social interaction. They mouth the bedding, their mother, toys; they discover about texture and taste and what can be digested and what cannot. They begin to carry items, or try to move and drag newspapers. They climb onto objects, learn to balance, co-ordinate eye, legs and tails, move objects with their feet, walk backwards and vocalise. They learn to distinguish sounds, remember and recognise routines that predict interaction with people or their mother approaching. They have already learnt her scent and can distinguish other dogs at 3 weeks old. Nature has designed them to learn how to use all their skills, and as they physically mature different skills need to be learned, until they become the fully functioning adults they have been wired to become.

If all the education and development was dependant on external reinforcement it is doubtful they would survive. Mother does not stand by applauding their achievements, they have a strong need to fulfil a learning desire. Sometimes their exploring backfires and they need the skill to remember what happened, sometimes this exploring leads to external reinforcement.

SPECIFIC INSTINCTS

At about 6–8 weeks breed specific instincts can be seen emerging. The Gordon puppies begin to point the chickens in the garden. The Border Collies begin to stalk each other. Given the right developmental opportunities these behaviours get stronger every time they are practiced. On many farms young collies are allowed to practice and refine their skills on the free range chicken or ducks before moving to larger stock.

Many people ask me about clicker training Border Collies to teach them herding skills. To the casual observer it seems that there is no reinforcement for the behaviours demonstrated. The dogs will learn four skills: go left, go right, stop, and walk directly in towards the sheep. The fifth cue is "that'll do" which is a learned skill; as the other partner in the activity leaves, the process stops being so reinforcing. If the collie had no formal training and was allowed to develop and play with their herding skills, most would push the prey into the corner of a field and hold them there all day. Their ultimate aim is to prevent movement, to take control. As the instincts are emerging the behaviour of working in partnership, either with another dog, pack or person, needs to be allowed to develop. Without that reinforcement of working together the youngster would become a sheep hooligan, pleasing themselves by running the stock for vandalism. The skill develops alongside partnering the teacher, if the teacher leaves the lesson, then the majority of the reinforcement from the activity will evaporate. If dogs were sticky leaving the training sheep, I used to go find another opportunity for working different sheep, or putting the hens to bed.

Of course a clicker can be used as you shape and refine the skills, the reinforcer is the continuation of the lesson. A young dog will often prefer certain skills to others, and you can increase the reinforcer value by cueing those behaviours. Using those instinctive skills will become more reinforced and stronger on every outing, until the dog can be regard as fixated on the stock. The speed of learning when teaching a young collie is nothing short of astonishing. They learn their stock, how they move when they flock, they begin to anticipate a change in balance that predict attempts to escape. They learn to read what the sheep are looking at, their weakness for grazing on the move, they fix their eye on the sheep but develop an awareness of your presence. They learn their land, their gateways, the vulnerable points in the fencing, they learn individual sheep and recognise stroppy behaviour and can even single out one of their own from a flock of strangers. (A common occurrence when fencing is not quite as good as it could be and next door is grazing handsome rams).

If the instinct is not developed along the usual route it can often find an alternative outlet. One of my Gordons pups that returned to me at four years old had no obvious birding instinct but can point a tennis ball at 6 feet and endure the fixation for over an hour. If she had the opportunity to develop the emerging instinct on birds, tennis balls would hold no attraction, but they make an excellent substitute that allows her instinctive behaviour to get strong and more reinforced. She shows an interest in chickens, but one bounce of the tennis ball and she returns to the behaviour that has the longest reinforcement history—working the ball. This reinforcement history is a key part of the puzzle, we can use it to our advantage.

There are a certain amount of instincts common to all dogs, and some of these develop to our advantage and some are inhibited. Watchfulness, or on duty behaviour, is common, where dogs alert to unknown noises or threats. Chasing small prey, such as squirrels or rats; sniffing the tracks of critters; making a bed; running for the love of running, going into water to swim. Dogs with strong tendencies for certain behaviour were bred together to develop

One of the most favoured breeds in the UK for Mountain Search and Rescue is the Border Collie. They are designed to function in the mountain environment. But this is the environment full of sheep which need to learn to be ignored when searching for people. To begin with the young collie is given many hours of play with the ball, tug or Frisbee and their trainee. The quantity needs to be sufficient that the instincts are stronger than any situation. If faced with greeting another dog, or going to eat the cue to play should exceed other interests. Once this level is achieved the activity is associated firstly with a field that has just been emptied of grazing sheep. The trainer will activate the youngsters around the smell of all that sheep poo. Secondly alongside a field of sheep on the other side of a fence, and then walking amongst the sheep. The long term training will involve the instinctive (play) activity as a reward for finding the person—who is predictably carrying the preferred toy in their pocket. Once the dog has united the missing person and trainer the chain of behaviours is reinforced by the high level activity that precedes the attendance of the broken leg.

The reinforcement history and its pattern around the scent and presence of sheep, stimulates the dog to see sheep as part of the cue to search for the person, holding the toy, that results in their favourite activity— mountain tennis.

genetically diverse instincts. I can see that the Border Collie stalk is rooted in the same behaviour as the point of the Setters, they are both predatory instincts. But the Collies instincts are triggered by the movement of the prey, and the Setters by the scent of the prey. The strength of the reinforcement when using these instincts is so strong that both breeds will find substitutes to allow their instincts to flourish. Kent (the Gordon) will fixate over the chickens, who never stay still so do not trigger the point, and Speck (collie) will try to herd the birds and bats, with his progeny using him as their sheep.

Also common to the breeds we choose to share our lives with is the instinctive need to interact. Without it dogs would behave similarly to cats or other solitary predators, but dogs have been bred for their need to live with people, and for some dogs this is extremely strong.

WHEN IT STOPS BEING A REINFORCER

Tiredness, both mental and physical can be easily covered by enthusiastic dogs. Puppies show they are tired with slower movements or simple fall asleep on the target mat. Using instinctive behaviours, particularly learning to use them, is quite exhausting. Nature designed dogs to be able to "run on vapour", particularly in the elements of the hunt behaviours. Feeling "a little tired", does not catch the dinner, sleep can happen afterwards. This is acceptable on occasion but would cause physical and mental damage if this tired state happened on every training session. There would also be a less than pleasant association with the behaviour under training.

When using instinctive behaviours remind yourself to stop before tiredness shows—by the time it is showing you have gone too far. Look out for the slightly slower reaction to your cues, markers and take up of the reinforcer.

INTERACTION

I consider this a primary reinforcer unless the behaviour has been inhibited during early development. My experience of street or village dogs is insufficient to assess whether they co-exist with people as a useful resource or need to be with people. I have meet several dogs rescued from a similar background, and with the exception of one all enjoyed, and chose, the company of people. Probably that was the behaviour that made their selection and expensive rehabilitation worth while. There are dogs that find interaction with people non-reinforcing and I would suggest that they come under specialised care where interaction becomes a learned and continually reinforced behaviour. For most normally reared and raised pet dogs interaction with the people in their lives is a primary reinforcer.

The type of interaction can be varied and have different impact. Baby puppies at 3 to 4 weeks of age do not like to be picked up unless they have a reinforcing association with the behaviour. But they do like the scent of human skin and faces, even before they begin to eat food. I lie on the floor on my stomach and allow the 3 week old pups to sniff my face and very quickly they begin to lick. This is often one of the first situations that stimulates a tail wag. Later when they are comfortable with being held and picked up the face licking can be used as a reinforcer for being picked up. Many dogs throughout their lives like to get close to our face, and even become specialists in face washing. It is a very usable reinforcer for these dogs. But if you were to offer your face for a lick and the dog was unknown, or keen to interact you could find your nose bitten off. This is a typical statement that I hesitate to use as an illustration because someone will not read the detail diligently and get bitten "because Kay said....." anyway it shouldn't happen twice as the punishment will either be attached to the proximity of their face near a strange dog, or they will learn to read more carefully or completely dismiss anything I have advised. That is the downside of punishment—you can never be sure which behaviour gets punished. My eldest Gordon, Mabel, has never licked my face, but does love to sniff my face, especially first thing in the morning when she hangs at the side of the bed for that first exchange of breath. So pleasant.

Licking a face is not a learned behaviour but an instinctive behaviour and part of later development of the desire for approval, this does not appear until about 5–7 weeks. If 3 week old pups are faced with a strange adult dog they behave very cautiously, crouch and return to their bed. At 6–7 weeks they greet the similar adult, through the puppy fence, with copious amounts of submissive approval-seeking behaviour. Many turn upside down, or show the inside of their back leg, lick their lips, whine, and may even urinate. This is the beginning of the development of their social skills. It would be dangerous to expose pups under this age to adults except their mother. If the learning of the approval seeking skill is underdeveloped, the only skill the pup has from their experience is to crouch and try to hide. You can begin to see that a rich learning environment appropriate to their developmental stage is essential. Pups that loose adult dog contact with early weaning, and then only interact with siblings may never develop approval seeking behaviour.

Having opportunities to socially interact is extremely important and reinforces the primary instinct. If a dog is reared without much contact with other dogs, their instinct to socially interact becomes focused on people, similar to the Border Collie instincts becoming fixed on balls instead of sheep. How you allow these self reinforcing instincts to develop and the patterns they are associated with, are extremely important to the way the behaviours are carried out for the rest of the dog's life.

A puppy will greet with excitement when recognising its family, particularly if this coincides with the end of solitary existence. Two elements add to the massively reinforcing moment: the end of solitary existence (they do not know you are going to return) and the re-bonding with their social pack. If you only greet the pup after they have been to the garden to pee, then this is the reinforcing pattern that will be established. My preferred choice when returning home is to let the dogs into the garden as soon as I arrive, and once they have slightly calmed down, become relieved that the pack is back together again, then I greet them individually. If I try to greet as soon as I come in the level of arousal exceeds their abilities for self control, and Gordon Setters jumping to eye level is more than any enthusiast should endure. I try to avoid both reinforcing events occurring together, and on some occasions in order to vary the routine I have returned, but not entered the house, dealt with other matters around the property and then greeted the dogs. The greeting was much more manageable. By establishing the pattern as pups, our social protocol becomes more strongly reinforced at every repetition.

All of the small elements of interaction can become strong reinforcers. If you enjoy playing with your dog, not only does the dog get reinforcement from using the instinctive hunting behaviours but also your focus and attention. Being the centre of your attention is highly reinforcing. Unfortunately the dogs' lifelong instinctive behaviour to learn and study us, leads to many different patterns of attention seeking evolving. Mabel achieved her first People's Master by removing my attention from the computer. As a pup she would tap the door to be let out, and coincidentally as soon as the door tapped, I stopped what I was doing and responded to her. Another example of the cluster of behaviours being reinforced—and not being able to be sure which behaviour the reinforcer attaches itself to. She still does the same behaviour now at 12 years old, or when I have my attention on visitors. At all other times she will wait with the others for a Door Open opportunity but my inattention triggers the door tap, reinforced by the attention. I often sit with visitors at the kitchen table who are hesitantly wondering if after the 15th tap "do you think she may want to go out....?" Once she settles by the door I go to open it, we observe through the

When collie pup Quick was 5 months old he needed to begin grooming, but since he was a very skin sensitive young man touching him with a brush or comb was not pleasant. My protocol was to elevate him onto a table so that he could lick my face, he is a very licky pup, and stroke him as if my hand was a brush. This was gold star heaven for him. The elevation to face level, the approving hand touches and being allowed to lick. The environment became reinforcing through the use of his instinctive need for social interaction and the approval. It took no time at all to introduce the brush with a hand stroke/brush stroke pattern and now the process of brushing him is reinforcing. If I am not paying attention he will quietly slip away demonstrating that the action of the brush on his coat is not the reinforcer. For any learned behaviour, but especially newly learned behaviours, the absence of the reinforcer will have an effect quickly.

window—she takes one sniff of the air, turns around to come straight back in. "aah.." Hmmm... some how I was "managed".

Mabel finds all attention extremely reinforcing. My hobby is heelwork to music and freestyle and I attempted several competitions with a young Mabel. Unfortunately early in her career one of those pesky Single Event Learning situations arose. Our routine was a Scottish Dance, with us both sharing full Gordon tartan regalia. She maintains a very elegant bow position and I performed dance steps around her, then I hold the position and she goes around me. On this S.E.L. occasion she missed the cue to go around me, and raised a titter from her audience. The pose lasted another 40 seconds before she moved, and all that time the audience was enjoying the "disobedience" more and more. From that date it was always risky to ask for a bow in any performance until the finale.

We demonstrated at the Gordon Setter championship show, and were greeted by a deeply awed audience "Gasp... she's off-lead". The final bow was held until the applause finally stopped, there was no separating her from her audience.

She very much enjoys free-shaping and demonstrating clicker training, with a noticeable "zest" to all her behaviours where an audience is responsive, and is known for creating entirely new behaviours only in that environment. Gordons have evolved a strong instinct to entertain and laughing people is more reinforcing than any offer of food. Which is quite a statement since they are gundogs with big appetites. Heaven help me if she found birds and an audience together.

MANAGING, THE POWER

Dogs spend their entire youth studying us for their first degree. Some become quickly proficient and continue to study for their Masters in People Management. Studying their environment is an instinctive behaviour, necessary for survival and constantly reinforcing. They need acute observation skills, memory and scenting abilities. They need to be able to notice very slight changes in their environment and be able to predict patterns of the prey and their predators. Small wonder that if they share a bedroom with you they can tell when you are rousing from your sleep by noticing the increase in your movements or recognise the alarm. They can see the excitement in your actions when you are planning to go out, or pack the suitcase. Murphy, used to go out to the car if I began to make sandwiches late at night—we must have a call out, and this was the only outcome of late night sandwich making.

We become key elements in their lives. We control their food, what they have, how much they have and when they have it. We control their exercise, and very often regular stimulation through training or games. We give them security and a sense of belonging to a group—all instinctive needs in most dogs. Being able to manage the powerful element in their lives is reinforcing.

Currently 5 dogs are floating around the garden, playing the game "My Toy is Better Than Yours". There are plenty of toys for each dog. What Speck has Dottie wants, so he teases her with his possession, enjoying the her absolute attention and the activities revolving around him. Something then distracts them and they all race to the fence to check it out. After this is evaluated Flink secures the toy but this has absolutely no effect on either Speck or Dot. Flink is younger and of little importance to them, and so stimulates no interest through possession of this toy. Within a minute this is dropped and Dottie snatches it to tease Speck. Speck and Dot are litter siblings.

Improving your level on the ladder is normal, and small, micro successes can be enormously reinforcing.

Perhaps the dog is lying in the doorway of the kitchen and with some difficulty you have to walk around them to leave the room. Firstly visualise your behaviour of walking from kitchen to sitting room without the door blockage. It would be upright, confident, relaxed. With the dog in the way you have to move more carefully, perhaps apologetically: "no, please don't get up", your balance is altered, you lose some relaxation. The dog, by being in this position and not moving, has managed to change your behaviour. Some dogs would NEVER notice, but those studying for their Masters will be writing notes. You need to be awake and smell the coffee, especially if this is a regular occurrence: it is being reinforced by the dog's instinct to manage their environment. You have reinforced this by the change in your behaviour. These very small, micro events can become so reinforcing that they begin patterns of more significant attempts.

This sounds rather like the dominance chestnut. I do not think dogs desire to dominate us, but discover through accidents, excellent observation and memory skills that they can manage us, sometimes to their own benefit, and sometimes because a response is better than no response. The outcome of the manipulation is often irrelevant, the dog in the doorway gained nothing from not moving, but the process of successful manipulation is highly reinforcing.

We can inadvertently reinforce dominating, or managing behaviour. Unfortunately the other side of this coin is the reinforcement enjoyed by the person who likes to be managed. "Oh darling, do you want me to take you for a walk?"

Kent is an 85 pound Gordon who is rather keen on greeting people. His youthful exuberance resulted in a eye level elevation in front your face. Most normal people learned to quickly take a step back to save their nose. Not being the sharpest knife in the drawer it took him a few months to notice and discover how really reinforcing it was to get people to step backwards for several paces when saying hello. Even if there was no overt reaction to this exuberance, that step backward movement was sufficient to maintain the leaping behaviour. He used to evaluate the sucker-rating of each visitor, attempt the power leap. If the visitor bravely continued without blinking (which takes some nerves of steel) he stopped the leaping.

Once passed into Second Stage of Greeting he likes to take hold of the bottom of your jacket. Many of my visitors are suitably dressed for dog greeting in fleeces with elasticated draw hems. These have a toggle for you to tighten the bottom of the jacket. Kent would grip these and DARE you to move away. If you ignored him he held his ground until the length of drawn out elastic started to ring warning bells in the wearer: "*this is going to hurt if he lets go*". To avoid such punishment the wearer would step towards him and after sufficient attention was given, usually in the range of 5 minutes of massage and luxuriating conversation, he would let go. Oops.

They key to avoiding subtle management is to make it appear like it was your idea all along, or practice indifference.

Not many of us deliberately try to teach our dogs to be dominate or be over managing but our desire to care for our dogs can be misread and the dogs can quickly develop an understanding that they are the centre of attention, and pretty much have all they desire. You may be the carer, but you can quickly turn into the servant by not paying attention to your own behaviour.

One desire for attention I deliberately magnify: when in pain—run to me for attention. Many years ago I assisted a friend to excavate her new German

Shepherd puppy from under their garden shed. The puppy had been playing in the garden and ran into a stone water bath. A bone in the toe was chipped, but the shock and pain drove the pup straight under the shed. I give any youngster that receives injury copious amounts of attention—I want them to react to pain, even mild pain, by running towards me.

You can plan to use your attention, or your laughter, as a reinforcer for so many of the tremendous behaviours that puppies offer you and shape their life long reactions.

You just need to "see with new eyes".

MIRRORING

I am in the enviable position of living with multiple dogs and I have been studying for my Dog Masters Degree for many years. I was also lucky to have a father who took every opportunity to reinforce my instinct to learn. I never heard the term "because I said so…" from him, I was given, the sometimes excruciatingly tedious, explanation with all the bells and whistles, which actually served the same long term desire—do what you are asked, and now.

I have also been lucky to be able to watch some exceedingly gifted trainers with their puppies and youngsters and one element I frequently see is the reinforcing power of mirroring. One dog will do something and the other dog will copy them or mimic. Speck collects a toy to run down the garden, all the others do the same. It is difficult to work out the reinforcer for the mimicker, but something must but be in operation there as the behaviour is well maintained. This also happens when people mimic the dog. A puppy starts to react excitedly—we react the same way, the pup rushes over to see that leaf and we react in the same way. The dog gets excited at arriving at the park, and we react in the same way (the excessive amount of hollering, anxious flustering movements, are interpreted by the dog as mimicking their state of arousal).

Your mirroring needs to be thought out and intentional. What you mimic will serve to reinforce the behaviour. Anxiety, arousal, interest, indifference, these can all be exaggerated by your reactions. Another friend of mine is a keen tracker, and with every new pup, without resorting to going along in the field on her hands and knees, she mimics the pup's behaviour of sniffing along tracks on the ground, showing great interest and focus. Another friend super-keen on obedience, always makes eye contact with her pups when they make eye contact with her. All her dogs spend many hours focussed on her—and it arises from just this reinforced "bud" as puppies. I have great friends or great resources?

I will return to this in more detail when I begin the chapter on applying these tools—but what is reinforced is what you get. When our junior dog class is teaching lead walking, I frequently query why they reinforced pulling in the first place? It is a strong branch of the mimicking tree.

PROXIMITY

This is part of the social security and power that many dogs find reinforcing. In the company of multiple dogs, the dog nearest to you is enjoying some reinforcement from their proximity to you over the other dogs. I keenly observe where each of the dogs settle when I change my activities. Often I place their bedding where they chose to settle, particularly for the dogs that find comfort a lower reinforcement than being nearest to me, or being able to watch me.

Speck and Dot, both collies, have comfort quite low of their list of favourite things and nearly always place themselves between me and the doorway out of the house. Any fun time tends to begin once I am through that doorway and they hate to miss out. Tessie will watch from her comfort until there is a definite cue for action—boots on, coat on, keys picked up.

CONNECTION

Tessie the youngest Gordon who returned to me at 4 years old, was very needy of my company for the first few months. As she became more confident she would watch me settle down to watch TV, and then go back to the kitchen to her favourite bed. This change in reinforcement need, was a good indicator of her change in sense of security. On odd occasions she "needs" to join me on the sofa, and perhaps something has happened during the day that has made her slight anxious. When I see her "needing" me more often, I take special care to have our staircase chats several times through the day. This frequent connection is deeply reinforcing for both of us, and reduces so much of the stress behaviours in all my dogs. It is sometimes easy to ignore the adults until their behaviour changes, this regular connection maintains a relaxed atmosphere and easily managed group.

The dogs will often chose how they maintain their connection with you. Quiz is 10 years old, very undemanding and is a comfort bunny. When I am working in the office, she captures Mabel's bed just outside the office, where she can hear me working. She can see the staircase if I leave, and about once or twice an hour will wander in look at me and then go back to bed. Mabel has by this time moved onto my bed, and again wanders in, but adds a "hrrmph" to express her opinion. Since she is now in her twilight years, I react to her

standing there with a micro break. After the early years of computer management activities, which took several traumatic months to undo, she has learned
to assess my concentration level. If I am involved in a "light" task, I am inter-
ruptible, if I am deeply wrapped up, she looks in, and walks away very
quickly. So skilled; I suspect she now has her PhD in Me.

This connection, the thread that binds the pack, is an invisible and easily
dismissible element. I see it more and more often, and feel greatly renewed
when the threads are strengthened. I see it in the elderly gentlemen taking his
dog for a walk. I see it in the casual hand contact between the farmer and his
tractor mate. I see it in the competitor resting their hand on their dog whilst
waiting to enter the ring.

The connection itself is difficult to observe until you have developed your eye
for the highly punishing disconnection that frequently occurs and is obviously
punishing behaviour. The person who has been training their dog, but continually casts around the room to see who is watching. The person who has been
playing with their dog but stops to talk to their friend. The disconnected walk
where the person and dog are physically separated and they are both
outwardly focussed: the dog is watching the horizon and the person is texting.
I see the dog, I see the withdrawal of the connection and a slice of understanding just evaporates.

Connection works at its best when equally reinforcing for both ends of the thread.

WHEN IT STOPS BEING A REINFORCER

Interaction can stop being reinforcing when the dog requires some "dog time".
Either to rest, sleep or interact with the ground. They need their own time, and
this is good time to absorb learning, who knows, perhaps they "reflect" on
their lessons! But without the down time from endless interaction and communication it can become a less effective reinforcer.

CHOICE

It was difficult to decide if choice is a primary or secondary reinforcer. It is
probably part of instinctive learning but I wanted to magnify its importance
since our inherited training and patterns of living with dogs often completely
strips the dog of being able to make choices.

Once of my course participants is a carer in a home for elderly folk. After we
talked about choice as part of the immeasurable power that our style of clicker

training encompasses, she changed her morning routine of getting the residents up and down stairs for breakfast. Instead of the pattern of deciding what they should wear, she gave each client a choice between two items of clothing, the pretty pink dress or the favourite green dress. What had become a difficult and stressful routine began to get quicker and quicker, and where practical became the policy for choice of food, choice of activity etc. It gives a sense of having control.

Too much choice can diminishing the ability to make the choice. One of my favourite restaurateurs re-vitalised their business by reducing their menu. Coming down from 14 main courses to choose from not only improved the menu reading time, but increased their turn over. Too much choice was daunting, minimal choice between A or B maybe sufficient to bring reinforcement to the activity. In the absence of reinforcement we are treading on grounds of punishment.

How many times does your dog rummage through their toy box to choose what to play with? One of my poor eaters improved his enthusiasm after being given first choice on the bones. They all looked the same to me, but a couple of minutes of sniffing and assessing each one perked up his appetite no end.

Many different types of clicker training have developed in the boom over the last ten years and it now demands us to describe what type of clicker training we employ. I am in total support of the free choice training, where the dog is give an object and allowed to choose their interaction. We look for error-less learning, with the dog making the choices along the error-less path. The power of choosing adds immeasurable reinforcement to the process of learning. Young puppies from 8 weeks old love to make choices, and thrive on this guided learning. Older dogs, and people, who have had their choices limited can struggle with making decisions. (to quote: "you'll have to tell me what to do"). I believe that given a choice the dog or person will stick with it for longer. When dealing with a problem I will set up the person with the opportunity to make the choice between solutions. By dictating what they should do there is a high risk of them not doing, not "buying into" it.

Having choice, and learning from choices, builds the learner. They acquire the skills of puzzle solving, the memory needs to provide barriers to poor solutions, and the ability to analyse is developed. Puppies of 12–16 weeks old are highly skilled in all these areas—use it or get used by it. The skills diminish through lack of use, and it is wonderful to see a dog blossom when they understand the concept of free shaping. The whole process, our devoted attention and focus, and the dog puzzling out how to get the click is immensely reinforcing.

SECONDARY REINFORCERS

A secondary reinforcer is an event or action that predicts a primary reinforcer. A click is a predictor, very often, of food. I have seen many dogs begin to salivate when they hear the click, and lick their lips.

If the click is used to mark the onset of play, the dog will become quite aroused when hearing the click. There is an emotional connection between the marker and the subsequent reinforcer.

For any secondary reinforcer, the connection can only be maintained through regular use, if the clicker is used and no reinforcer follows the effect of the click will diminish.

When training puppies I whistle as I take their food to their pen, from 4 weeks. Initially they don't look up but begin to scan the floor for the food, after about 5–7 days they look up for their individual meals or treats. At any time I can whistle to arouse them and they will run to the source of the whistle. This is always reinforced with food when they arrive, and at 6 weeks their mouths start to "nibble" in anticipation of the meal when they hear the whistle.

The pairing between the marker and the reinforcer, or punisher, can happen between any predictable (and unpredictable) event and any reinforcer. It very often happens without our realising it. As a training tool it is invaluable to be able to reinforce away from the behaviour. If the dog has moved or jumped in a way I want to reinforce, I can click, and give the food when the dog has moved to a new or appropriate location. When the Gordon turns towards you on the whistle—you click, interrupting their browsing is a seriously good achievement, and the reinforcer can be delivered where it suits. The pairing does not thrive when the time delay creeps up over 2/3 seconds. But in the case of a recall over 100 yards, the marker can be delivered for leaving the rabbit and when the dog looks at you, you can visually begin to reinforce through getting the treat bag out, rummaging around and by the time the dog arrives have chosen the best sausage. If the dog is familiar with your routine of selecting sausages, then as they see you begin the pattern, the behaviour of moving towards you will be being reinforced.

When training my dogs in a group I use eye contact as the marker. I give the cue for a sit, as each dog arrives and sits, I look directly at them and follow with the food. If we are walking on lead, the dog that moves to my side gets marker with a touch, and the walk sets off. We may be standing watching some activity. If my dog remains calmly at my side, with no need to commentate, another touch, followed by food or affection.

Secondary reinforcers are often referred to as "bridges", between the behaviour and the reinforcer, and can work similarly with punishers.

In class there may be 8 handlers working on different exercises with their dogs. As I wander around the room to check on progress, I may stop to ask a question or give feedback. The anticipation of me stopping or watching an individual can put them into a state of anxiety. This usually is evidenced in their complete disconnection to their dog and loss of focus. My approach or proximity can quickly become a bridge to the subsequent punisher and the behaviour at that time will diminish.

I rarely see anyone deliberately set up a bridge with a punishment, but it happens alarmingly regularly without intention.

LEARNED REINFORCERS

Additionally new reinforcers can be built by pairing with primary reinforcers. Some dogs find stroking difficult to accept, but when paired with the delivery of food, it can become a pleasant, and eventually reinforcing activity. To counter the punishing effect of stroking will depend on to what degree the stoking is unpleasant. It will be a strong reinforcer, used on many hundreds of occasions to make a difference. In some cases it will need pairing for life, since in the absence of the primary reinforcer the dog moves away from the touch. It would suggest that the activity is a primary punisher.

But we can associate many different activities with primary reinforcers to enable easy interaction with the dogs. We are inclined to use the term "good boy" or "good girl" to reward the dog, but unless the way you use that expression has been paired with a primary reinforcer it is meaningless to the dog. It may make us feel better as we believe we have rewarded the dog, but unless the behaviour increases, we haven't.

The only way to measure whether the pairing has been sufficient to make the second activity reinforcing is to take away the primary reinforcer and use the learned reinforcer, as a reinforcer.

Unfortunately we accidentally pair many incorrect behaviours with correct behaviours. The dog jumps up to greet, and then sits, and the sit gets reinforced. If the jump keeps repeating itself, it has not been punished by simply choosing the correct behaviour to reinforce. You may THINK you have ignored the jumping, but unless you removed your attention, walked out the room, broke the connection, you may not have punished the behaviour. This is back to the distinction between reward and reinforcement. If the unwanted behaviour continues, it is getting reinforced, your intention is irrelevant. In the situation of this incorrect/correct pattern the whole pattern is reinforced. See chapter* for more detail of this process)

KNITTING

Reinforcers and punishers are threading their way through all our behaviours. It is the nature of behaviour to change, and the outcomes of these changes are memorised, or we make the same mistakes repeatedly. The outcomes will either maintain or fade the behaviour depending on whether they are reinforcing or punishing.

But behaviour rarely happens in isolation. Several behaviours can happen at the same time and reinforcers and punishers can be attached to the wrong element. The dog may bark at the back gate, and be punished by a spray of water. The association can be made with the location, being at the back gate, the stranger walking by, (and the dog now becomes even more anxious when they hear the approach of strangers), or the barking, or you holding a bowl of water. You can only look for evidence of the affect of the punisher on the behaviour that diminishes.

You think you are reinforcing the paw wave, the dog is in the sit position. When you cue the dog to shake a paw when he is standing there is no response. There is no reinforcement history for that behaviour—the paw wave AND the sit, have been paired and only reinforced together, not in isolation.

We teach the dog to drop (down), this is usually achieved somewhere near our feet. When given the cue around the other side of the sheep the dog returns to your feet to drop. What is reinforced is what will be strengthened. What is reinforced is the entire pattern of behaviours, location, speed, pace, and emotion.

Behaviours connected with the reinforcing behaviours can feel the "wash" of the reinforcer, particularly where the reinforcer is strong. Part of our skill in using reinforcers effectively is to make very sure which behaviour they attach to.

YOUR REINFORCEMENT

Begin to become aware of what reinforcement you get out of the process of training or enjoying your dog. This may vary from the pleasure of seeing your dog alert and interactive, or it may come from the approval of other people when you demonstrate the final behaviour. It may come from both, but if one part of the teaching process is higher in reinforcement than the other you will become biased and effective at that element at the expense of the other. I have many learners in both camps—the inveterate teacher of new behaviours that never finishes a behaviour, and the over hasty trainer who puts the behaviour on cue too soon so that they can show off the final result.

We have learners who inadvertently reinforce undesirable behaviours. Either because the dog is mirroring them, their state of anxiety or stress; or they receive more social attention from friends and experts when their dog has a "problem".

Become aware of your own reinforcer, and manage it.

PUNISHERS

We cannot avoid them and we all use them. A punisher is just the term used to measure the outcome. A behaviour has been "punished" because the behaviour diminishes, fades or happens less frequently. Very often we will simply remove the reinforcer, or opportunity for reinforcement and encourage the behaviour to fade in its own time. For positive trainers there is a similar misuse of the term "punish" as "reward", we get stuck on the intent of the deliverer, and not measuring the outcome of either on the behaviour. As soon as our head, and our heart, is around that distinction we can become very effective in using reinforcement and punishment without ever diminishing the dog, or our relationship.

Jumping up at people is a juvenile behaviour. If the opportunity for careless reinforcement is avoided, the pup is maitained at floor level through the greeting process and NEVER reinforced for elevating, then the behaviour of trying to jump for attention will not be reinforced, and not develop. Dogs are so much more skilled than people at becoming aware of the outcome of a single event. You have to be on your toes through all interactions with young animals, and ruthless in managing the behaviour of other people. One careless visitor, who "doesn't mind" the puppy jumping up at them (I wonder about why that is reinforcing huh?), can make a lifetime of bad habits. I will cover the reinforcement patterns in Chapter 5 but briefly, in my experience when an instinctive behaviour is allowed to be reinforced on just one occasion, the dog will continue to attempt success in that behaviour many hundreds of times. On the other hand, if a learned behaviour is only successful once, and the success is not repeated many hundreds of times, it usually fades instantly. The key to the fading rate relative to the reinforcement schedule is the instinct vs learned behaviour. Using that instinctive behaviour does not need external reinforcement.

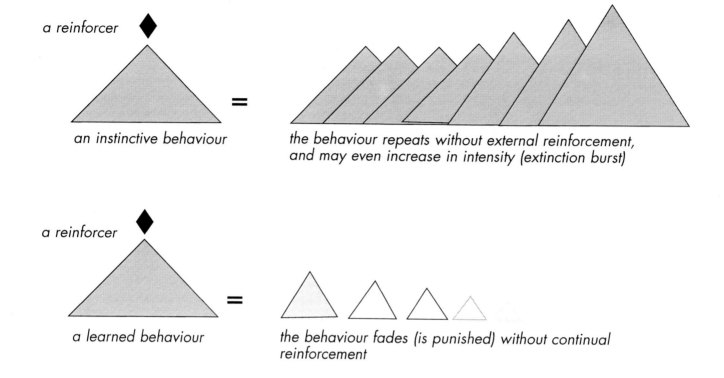

a reinforcer ◆

an instinctive behaviour   =   *the behaviour repeats without external reinforcement, and may even increase in intensity (extinction burst)*

a reinforcer ◆

a learned behaviour   =   *the behaviour fades (is punished) without continual reinforcement*

I have access to exercise my dogs on stock free farm land. Quite often deer cross our path, and neither of my breeds are fast running chasers. The young collies spy their first galloping deer and take off, returning a few minutes later, tongue lolling out. An unsuccessful instinctive response, the deer can outstrip both Collie and Gordon with ease. Next occasion, the youngster doesn't even take breathe to chase when they see a deer—the behaviour has extinguished, instantly This is especially effective on the first occasion of the behaviour. Lack of success was a punisher, and for the collies they learn the same reaction with hare and pheasant. When they notice the deer they are inevitably busy using their herding instinct on their peers. This is a highly, and continuously reinforcing activity which is the norm for our exercise. To break from this behaviour and react to the deer, it would be a double value punisher. Firstly because they are not fast enough to catch the deer, and secondly because they ended a reinforcing behaviour—herding their peers.

Perhaps if we were on a more relaxed walk, where there is very low value reinforcer for the collie—just browsing the hedges, deer chasing would be more reinforcing in comparison. This is touching on the value of reinforcers covered in Chapter 3.

The Gordons have no reaction to deer or hare, but live to point the birds. Pheasant and partridge sit tight when they hear 85 pounds of predator crashing through the undergrowth. Without excellent scenting skills they would miss the birds but the many generations of selective breeding has fine tuned the discriminating skills and they freeze as soon as they get the scent of the bird. The freeze is instantly transferred to any Gordon within visual reach. This is referred to as "backing", and dogs are assessed for this essential skill in trials. Without the instinct to back, No.2 dog could carelessly crash into the birds if the wind was not carrying the scent to their location. The backing dog usually faces the pointing dog, not the location of the bird unless they also have the scent. The pointing dog now needs to hold the point until responding to the cue to flush. My dogs are not trained for shooting, so they respond as they choose on point. Kent over-freezes, and will stand quite still for several minutes. Mabel will very slowly, catlike, move one leg at a time to approach the prey—with every intention of going for a kill. For her this is a self taught, technique successful in 2001, and still employed today, in 2008, although she has never caught a bird since the first occasion in 2001.

Interestingly the collies never respond to the Gordon's point and vice versa. Both breeds back each other in stalking behaviour, but it does not cross the breeds. The collies usually serve the role of pheasant crashing to break Kent from his freeze.

TYPES OF PUNISHERS

Most of the punishers we employ will be the removal of the reinforcer. Tessie is fixated on balls, especially those that squeak. At times this serves a useful purpose, where she "points", or fixates, on the ball for a couple of hours, just shifting position every few minutes. Obviously a highly reinforcing behaviour needing no external reinforcement, she does not need anyone to interact with the ball to increase the pleasure. Occasionally a fast collie will steal the ball, and it usually takes her a few minutes to realise what has happened, she does not chase the collie with the ball or fixate or point to it. But if the ball enters the house the behaviour goes into high arousal, and this needs to be managed. We have a successful (from my viewpoint) technique of removing the ball "to go to bed", where it is placed in a basket in the cupboard. The fixating behaviour has been "punished", I need to seal the ball inside a plastic bag, or the scent of the ball through the edge of the cupboard door will trigger fixation to the cupboard. In this behaviour the cue and the reinforcer are the same.

I also use this cue/reinforcer to avoid another behaviour. When out on a walk Tessie will harass Mabel, who is now too old for these politics, so the ball comes along for the walk, and relieves the stress for Mabel, keeping Tessie fully employed. Managing this reinforcer, manages the occurrence of the behaviour.

Very, very often the punishers and reinforcers are two sides of the same coin. You can withdraw attention and give attention, one will punish the behaviour, one will reward it. It is extremely difficult to be neutral. And like reinforcers, punishers have different values, can be continuous, and are hard to ensure the attach to single behaviours.

AMBIGUOUS INFORMATION

This is one area that probably causes more behaviour to break down than any other single punisher when working with positive reinforcement. We perceive ourselves as working in an environment where we only want to reinforce behaviour and we avoid aversive or deliberate punishment. But our own lack of self discipline cause effective punishment when we fail to communicate clearly what is required, and whether it is correct or not. We default to using words, which dogs find hard to discriminate between, and contradict what we say with how we use our body language.

We stand at the door telling the dog to go outside, but our body language clearly states that we have no intention of going outside. Which is the dog to believe?

We tell the dog to stop barking but our agitation clearly tells the dog there is something amiss.

We tell the dog "good boy" but our dissapointment clearly tells the dog we are frustrated, possibly with ourselves, but we "taint" the intended reinforcement.

Behaviour begins to "bloom" when the communication is clear, without doubt and easily understood.

THE TOOLS

The variety of different reinforcers and punishers available to us is extensive. The repertoire is often very individual, what is reinforcing for one person is not for another and the same for dogs, and what reinforces a behaviour in one situation does not in another.

Our second step is to learn the tools of using the reinforcers to affect the results we desire.

3 Tools: Using Reinforcers

"The way positive reinforcement is carried out is more important than the amount."

B.F. Skinner 1969

During my self reinforcing, instinctive, behaviour of People Watching, especially dog trainer watching, I observe some excellent techniques where multiple reinforcers are used to great effect. These often become known by training methods, copied extensively with varying success. Pre-clicker days we used to teach a dog to walk backwards, backing, with a tug toy. The dog would be fully engaged on gaining ground whilst tugging, and when the person allowed the dog to pull them, the dog moved backwards. Adding a cue to the movement would eventually result in the movement without the toy to gain the toy, and reinforcement through the game with the toy that followed. It was mostly successful, but could take some time to establish the new verbal cue since the tug was the cue itself. When taught this way the final behaviour can be very fast and exciting from the high state of arousal that the game encouraged, and this state of arousal would be locked into the behaviour. A lot of our training techniques originated from gifted people who observed behaviour happening during play (read: learning interaction) and captured those behaviours.

Today I prefer to use the clicker with a food reinforcer to allow the dog to explore the movement and self teach. This is a slower road to the final behaviour, but that slowness allows me to intervene if the behaviour starts to "wobble" or in the case of backing, usually goes off line. Behaviours that require a high degree of accuracy and understanding are best taught slowly with precision and diligence. I can then choose to add more arousal by changing the reinforcer, or calm the behaviour similarly. The skill is established, the reinforcer, when predicted, changes the intensity of the behaviour. When teaching with the toy-n-tugging the intensity was fixed. First learning will have an impact on the behaviour for life, if the first learning is calm, assured, relaxed and accurate, at any time you can revert to this format of the behaviour.

When teaching this "method" there is a multiple range of reinforcers, associations and several behaviours happening at the same time. With an extremely powerful reinforcer such as toy tugging; using the instinctive behaviour of killing, or de-gloving, (the tug), interacting with you (the provider and powerful entity), and your reactions by allowing them to successfully tug you, you would have to be 100% able to ensure errorless learning. With this amount of power flowing into strengthening the behaviour when things go off track they quickly become fixed and extremely hard to correct. The dogs move backwards off centre, or do not use their legs equally, moves in an erratic way, they may put their feet on you for extra leverage, they could be vocalising, which may become barking when the toy is not in their mouth, they could loose control with over arousal and not be able to respond to cues.

It is the complexities that can severely diminish the effectiveness of the reinforcer. I have seen really delicious treats have little effect on improving the behaviour. I have seen toy training diminish the sparkle on every repetition. I have seen dogs wander off after reinforcement, reluctant to return to the behaviour. Why? Several mixtures can be causing the loss of effectiveness:

◆ The reinforcer is of a lesser value than expected.

◆ Normally when the dog returns to you at the run they get a great treat. Today you are treat-less, worried about financial matters, unfocussed and simply put the dog on the lead.

◆ You are free shaping a new behaviour but the dog loses focus and wanders off.

◆ Your expectations are so high, that despite the click and treats for each success, the effort of trying to work out exactly what it is you want depresses the dog's desire to try. Your disappointment in them not "getting it" shows in your body language.

◆ The dog leaves the start line with low enthusiasm.
You are teaching your dog to hold the start line and using the toy to reinforce the waiting. But your game is more suited to the 60lb Labrador that taught you this technique than the young 30lb spaniel who finds you games rather too violent and brain shaking.

◆ The dog performs in a flat and disinterested manner when in competition. In practice the dog receives great treats with high frequency for each behaviour. But in the competition experiences no treats zero reinforcement and a punishing interaction because the handler has gone into Ring Zombie.

These examples are not the only solutions to the changes in behaviour, but you can quickly see how the reinforcer, or its misuse, can warp the behaviour. You may think you are reinforcing but only the performance of the behaviour can dictate that, not your intent.

I'm going to throw two of my favourite B.F. Skinner quotes at you to consider:

1. "The way positive reinforcement is carried out is more important than the amount."

2. "....what is inherited is not the behaviour but a susceptibility to reinforcement."

I suggest that a behaviour that has been built, or taught, through careful and effective reinforcement is strong, maintained but also very susceptible to the reinforcer, AND ANY CHANGES TO IT.

Back in the olden days, which I remember with sadness, the dogs struggled through punishment based teaching. The punishment was consistently effective at preventing the unwanted behaviours. It certainly didn't teach the dog how to perform the wanted behaviour with joy, passion or pleasure, just how to avoid your displeasure or aversive handling. What remained was, hopefully, the behaviour you wanted. In situations where there was no opportunity to punish, perhaps in competition or off lead, you were left with the residue, desired, behaviour and this was seen to be consistent.

Now we focus on reinforcement training we leave ourselves vulnerable to the reinforcer and its pattern, pulling and straining the behaviour. The reinforcement pattern is strongly wrapped around the behaviour, and can easily distort it.

To begin to understand the reinforcement process, and the elements that contribute to the effectiveness I want to begin with the simplest series of events.

JUMPING UP TO GREET

For most people, at some time, this is an undesirable behaviour. Personally I will not encourage un-cued jumping, but am quite willing for the dogs to place their feet on me when cued. I am not content for them to presume to try this behaviour on visitors.

The ABC of behaviour:

Antecedent = something happens that triggers the behaviour.
This can be external: a person saying hello or bending over, or internal: a desire for attention. Both of the antecedents are cues.

Behaviour = this is what happens.
Feet are placed on, or dug into, a person, their legs or shoulders.

Consequence = this affects whether the behaviour happens again or not, gets stronger or weakens.
Something the dog finds pleasurable will reinforce the behaviour, make it likely to happen again or make it stronger. Something unpleasant should weaken or fade the behaviour.

Puppies jump up naturally, people do not teach it. The pups will jump at their dam, get highly reinforced when they place their feet on the bitch from about 4 weeks as they suckle from her when she is standing. Think how many minutes of their very short time awake is spent in this very pleasurable, rein-forcing position. Even behind a fence, and having never been given attention for the behaviour the pups will stand up with their feet on the fence.

It is then a natural progression when interacting with very large bodies; people, that the pups at some time will place their paws on the person. If this behaviour is reinforced with interaction, attention or food, it will increase in frequency and strength at an alarming rate. It may only take 3 accidental repetitions of the reinforcement for it to become a highly fixed, instinctive behaviour. It will take many, many months to re-pattern the dog to greeting without paw contact.   .

Even with 5 week old puppies the reinforcer can be delivered when not jumping. They are unlikely to analyse the lack of attention, they are too young, but we can take the reinforcer to a location where the only way to enjoy the reinforcer is to stay on the floor. The attention and hand contact can prevent the jumping or food arriving at face level.

This is the pattern we are looking for:

> Antecedent = person saying "hello", eye contact, or bending over

> Behaviour = maintaining floor contact with front feet, maybe a sit

> Consequence = person bends down, focus, attention, a fuss, a treat

Since the behaviour of making paw contact originates in an instinctive behaviour, it will revert to this behaviour when there is insufficient reinforcement for the alternative. Ignore the well behaved, sitting puppy, just once and there is a very high risk they will paw contact for attention.

But this is the usual pattern:

> Antecedent = desire for attention from the puppy, interest—what is happening over my head? Person bending over arouses puppy or aroused people "pull" the puppy upwards.

Behaviour = paw contact

Consequence = high levels of attention, mimic arousal, interaction

We must also consider the second player in this scenario, the person:

Antecedent = puppy face, large eyes, desire to touch and hold

Behaviour = arousal, smiling, talking in a puppy voice, hands touching

Consequence = puppy adoration, excitement, extreme pleasure.

And so the circle goes around.

There is usually a third party in the scenario—the owner of the puppy. They will get reinforcement from the attention to their puppy, and be unable to simply say:

"No, do not let my puppy jump on you."

"Oh, I don't mind." Yeah sure, until the next time you visit and he weighs 70lbs and you are wearing your posh frock ... then you will mind! (They may even use this behaviour as a reinforcer for their need for social contact and approval.)

This behaviour may not be inappropriate in young puppies, but there will be more than one occasion where it will be undesired: when wearing delicate clothes, or bare skin. Puppies can have sharp nails, or be quite normal over boisterous puppies around vulnerable people. Certainly large adult dogs can be more than a nuisance jumping at people when unwanted.

But the pattern that maintains a strong counter-instinctive behaviour is a bit of a bother, you have to bend over, and the back isn't quite up to that any more, you may be in a hurry, or not paying attention and it is just easier not to bother about it on this one occasion. As with all instinctive behaviour, if it gets reinforced once in one hundred occasions, that one possibility of reinforcement will ensure the dog keeps trying for the next occasion. The perfect intermittent schedule increasing the behaviour—rather like gambling, perhaps this next one will be the winner. It will take hundreds of reinforcers on the non-instinctive behaviour, of standing under control, or sitting, to ensure it maintains. That instinctive desire to jump up will never disappear, the behaviour of non-jumping will need a life-long history to be susceptible to reinforcement. With the Gordons I took a side route. They all become very highly aroused when greeting and I allowed jumping with the rule that they must not touch the person. I like to see them happy and containing them to feet on the floor behaviour was not the reason I enjoy Gordons.

What seemed a nuisance behaviour is going around in a continually reinforcing cycle, and needs diligence and attention to prevent constant re-occurrence. But when you greet your dog who does not have that extra 60 seconds to give them the focus they deserve as a reinforcer for the behaviour you can live with? The guests (usually who should know better) need to be clearly told what to do and how to behave around your puppy. Then you can find an easy way to reinforce their consideration and forethought with a cuddle (where you pick the pup up to give to them), or teach the youngster a trick they can perform for visitors. This can be a highly effective reinforcer for the visitors, especially when they get to deliver the treat.

Wading through these patterns can take some experience and practice at employing reinforcement to match the results you want. You will need to develop good observation and analysis skills to accurately pair behaviours with their reinforcers.

How you use the reinforcer, which reinforcer, what quantity, what frequency and where it happens all affect the behaviour, and these are your tools.

1. WHERE: THE LOCATION OF THE DELIVERY OF THE REINFORCER

Just as punishment can be associated with a location, so can reinforcement.

Tessie arrived from a single dog household, and had no social skills at eating times. I feed my dogs raw bones on most occasions, and initially the proximity of other dogs was an aid to get her to tuck into the novel bones rather than play with them. When you've been kibble fed for four years bones take extra work. After a couple of months this turned around and the proximity of the collies became an excuse to have theirs as well as hers. Now she eats behind a gate. When preparing the food, Tessie recognises the pattern of my cues, and immediately takes herself to "her spot". This is the location of the delivery of the reinforcer—dinner. When I pick up a lead, she goes to the front door, this is the location of the reinforcer, yes, we are going for a walk, she also does the same when I put boots on. My colleague Mary Ray has a collection of dogs who all go to the front door when they hear her use the hair spray—that tells you something about her routines when leaving the house.

These patterns of the reinforcer arriving at the same location can be used to your advantage or can become the detractors of the behaviour you are trying to achieve.

Through this Chapter I am going to suggest some exercises you can try. Becoming effective in using these tools will be greatly increased if you take each tool individually and use them with different reinforcers, and learn to observe how they affect the behaviour.

EXERCISE 1: DINNER TIME

If you do not already, for one week, make sure you go through exactly the same pattern to prepare your dog's dinner. Give lots of verbal cues, converse with the dog, give them attention, involve them in the process. When ready, place the bowl in a different spot than your usual routine. Even at a rate of one meal a day by the end of seven days you should see the dog begin to anticipate this location, and head towards it as you pick up the bowl. This anticipating behaviour is then reinforced, because, sure enough, down comes the bowl.

EXERCISE 2: GOING FOR A WALK

If you have a going-for-a-walk pattern, see if you can change the location of leaving the house, or ask the dog to wait at the bottom of the staircase before you put the lead on. In this case the lead going on is a marker that promises the primary reinforcer of hunting (going out, checking the scents of prey, marking, scenting, running, playing, chasing). Dramatise your preparation routine, then take yourself and the lead to the new spot. Just wait quietly for the dog to join you, cue a sit, or controlled wait whilst you clip the lead on. Then proceed to the exit. This is a good technique that enables you to manage the approach to the exit. If the arousal of putting the lead on and going out the door are close together it becomes difficult to manage the reinforcers for both behaviours at the same time.

EXERCISE 3: VISITOR ROUTINES

You will need an extra body or two to help with establishing this. On the cue of the doorbell ringing, take the dog with you to The Station. You can practice this before the door bell is introduced, by rattling the treat box at a specific location, preferably away from the visitors arriving point, perhaps the kitchen. Then arrange for a friend to spend 15 minutes at your door. They ring the bell, you go to the station where the food box is waiting, rattle the box, and give several treats over a one minute period. Leave about 5–10 seconds between each treat, keeping the dog in location with lots of focus and your attention. After the minute, go back to your previous task, or invent several tasks and wait for the next door bell ring, or gate opening, or what ever precedes the chaos of arriving visitors. You can set up a time interval with your "ringer" where they ring once every five minutes, and practice the go to The Station routine.

What will begin to happen as the dog anticipates their reinforcer station, they will become reinforced for recognising the cues and anticipating the activity by heading for the station on hearing the doorbell.

This is a counter-instinctive behaviour. It would be normal for the dog to back you up to greet visitors, or the threat, since at that time your focus and arousal is fixed at the door location. Backing up the pack, joining in the arousal of answering the door is all part of an instinctive behaviour. Going away from this location to a station is counter-instinctive and the self reinforcer of using an instinctive behaviour will always be stronger. Absence of a reinforcement at your preferred Station, will weaken or extinguish the behaviour very quickly. This is a lifetime reinforcement pattern.

EXERCISE 4: TEACHING SIT TO HEEL

Most of us teach a puppy to sit in front of us. It is easier—you can see the pup clearly, there is a natural inclination for the pup to look up at the face or food and this triggers a change in balance that encourages the sit. Plenty of practise at this, for food or for greeting attention or for dinner will ensure a reliable response.

But now we want to progress to the dog sitting at our side, or to heel. We have become to believe that the dog "knows" sit. Sure, when they are in front of you, they respond to the cue "sit". But at your side there is no reinforcement history of that behaviour. What often happens when the dog hears the "sit" they move to the front of you and sit. If the lead is held tight preventing this change of location, then the dog may not respond at all. Don't blame the dog, the behaviour is moulded by the reinforcement pattern.

Begin with the cue for the dog to sit, and after they have sat, move yourself into a heel position by the dog, then reinforce. This "explains" that reinforcement for the sit happens in other places, and varies the reinforcement location. Once this has been sufficiently established the dog will respond in the heel location. You will know when this has been established by the response of the dog, uncertainty or excessive hesitation means you still have an imbalance of the reinforcement location, and need to continue reinforcing by delivering the treat, in the heel position, and perhaps never treating in the in front position until the new location has an effect on the behaviour.

EXERCISE 5: TEACHING DOWN AT THE DISTANCE

Similarly to the sit to heel exercise, the reinforcement pattern for the down or drop has been in close proximity to you. When cued out of reinforcement location, the dog will be confused, or try to get to the reinforcement location. Build up a pattern of reinforcing the dog at the distance—for nothing more that just being at the distance. Using large, visible treats, toss them over the dog's head before they have time to return to you. Use the same hand action and the dog will begin to anticipate the location and hold their location. When this is predictable try the cue for the down.

When building these location behaviours you can begin to evaluate the power of the reinforcer. The more powerful the reinforcer for the dog, the faster the dog will seem to "learn" the pattern. It is one of several methods to evaluate the reinforcer hierarchy.

I teach my dogs to back up away from me for a Freestyle behaviour. This is taught with a target mat. The click marks arrival on the mat and I reset the behaviour by reinforcing the dog in the opening position, which is in front of me. If the dog performs a good movement, but stops short of the mat, there is no reinforcer, and they will come back to the opening position to try again. One of our talented trainers taught her greyhound an excellent backing behaviour, but always reinforced at the outcome, ie; the distance the dog achieved. The click stops the dog and Caroline walks towards the dog, or throws the food for a catch. In this case if Elsa does not get a click, she stays where she is.

Neither method is right or wrong. This is just an illustration how the location of the delivery of the reinforcer, affects the behaviour in the event of non-success. The dog is attracted to the location of the reinforcement pattern. We start to see that although the click powerfully communicates what behaviour earned the subsequence reinforcer, the reinforcer itself shapes the behaviour. The behaviour is not a fixed occurrence in time, the whole pattern of preparation, movement, location, marker, reinforcer, emotional involvement is also rein-forced, and must be considered.

When the reinforcer is always delivered in the same location as the click, I have seen dogs learn to use that delivery point as part of the information. It does raise the question whether the click is required at all. It is a marker with precision and minimal duration, it does not require movement. But with behaviours close to the reinforcer delivery, it is questionable whether the dog is learning from the click or from the delivery.

Example: Dog is cued to sit, click, food delivered to the dog whilst in the sit. Dog holds the sit position. Dog is then cued to down, click, food delivered to the dog whilst in the down. This dog will hold position on the click, waiting for food to be delivered. This technique is very advantageous to maintain immobility or duration of an achieved outcome. The same technique could be used for the target mat, food delivered to the dog whilst on the mat or a contact point. But there is a disadvantage if you wish to practice the behaviour that results in the outcome: ie; the action of sitting a particular way, the action of running to the mat, the action of moving into the down. When only the outcome is marked, the method to reach the outcome can be varied. It also requires a linking behaviour of finishing one behaviour to be able to practice again. It seems clumsy.

The opposite scenario is to click for the sit, but feed in a variable location: toss the food away, or draw the dog back to the standing position. If you fix the food delivery location it will become paired with the behaviour. For instance a sit to heel can be clicked, but the dog fed when setting off. The two behaviours will lock together. Variety in the food delivery or reinforcement delivery will give greater focus to the click, and the reinforcer will become paired with the learning event, not a specific location. I keep food in either hand, any pocket or treat bag, on a table, and deliver in many, many locations.

Your choice of where you reinforce must be considered. Do not only focus on what you click, but the location of the reinforcer must compliment the behaviour you are seeking, not detract from it, and make the dog work outside its understanding.

In conclusion: if you want a behaviour to happen in a specific place, at the kerb, by the door, in the ring, near the other dogs, then you must first establish this environment as a place with a good, strong reinforcement history. Deliver a high schedule of reinforcement at that location, before you begin to cue learned behaviours.

This is experienced by many trainers, who have superb, finished behaviours in a particular environment: the home, the garden, the club, but see a dramatic drop in quality at other locations. With a young dog intended to perform in a variety of places, then the variety of places MUST have a strong reinforcement history. Even the driveway, the local park, the ringside, must be inclusive if you can visualise requiring first class behaviours in that environment.

2. WHERE: THE LOCATION OF THE REINFORCER BEFORE DELIVERY

This can make or break the success of a behaviour. The dog that has a good history of treat or play training will become familiar with the location of your store of reinforcers.

For example: I always teach my collies to drop: take up the down position at speed, with the spine dropping level, by using a tug toy. I particularly want this as a fast responding, aroused behaviour, and the dog to maintain the position tense and ready for action or the reinforcer: tugging. It is not the settled, lie down, that is suitable for the living room or resting by my chair—that is "down", and taught with food, a fuss, a belly rub. If I stand up holding the tug at waist height the dog is required to physically move away from the reinforcer, toy, to be able to enjoy the game. This can be really hard when teaching the behaviour, but an excellent self control exercise once well taught.

To teach this I will sit on the floor playing tug with my hands at floor level. When I see the dog responding dropping slightly to increase their power to tug, I will click, or mark it, and reinforce with an extra shaking session or even let go to allow the dog to win. Soon this "winning" strategy gets stronger, and more predictable. I particularly use the tug for this behaviour since the dog's balance when pulling is low and backwards—the ideal momentum for the drop behaviour.

Once the behaviour is predictable as I drop the tug lower, I will cue the behaviour before the dog gets hold of the tug, click, and use the game as the reinforcer. But when I move to the standing position the dog can easily become pulled by the higher tug and not respond to the drop cue, or respond slowly, and not complete the behaviour. They have learned the behaviour in relation to the position of the tug, which is wrapped up in the cue. The location of the much anticipated reinforcer acts as a counter-lure to the behaviour, and the reinforcing game usually happens out of the behaviour. All this contributes to lowering the quality of the behaviour. You must be vigilant that you only reinforce perfection, and that you only very gradually change the location of the pre-reinforcer and the game. If you see a lowering of quality, it is likely you have changed one of the locations too quickly.

We often train with our, or technically the dog's, reserve of treats near by. I am absolutely sure that all treat trained dogs begin to learn where there reserve is kept after watching you prepare, store and travel with "their treats". For some dogs this can be an important resource and assuring its safety in all conditions become a distraction to their learning. In a mixed training environment where other dogs are constantly moving around, the dog may need to feel protective over their reserve. This can also transfer to a favourite toy placed on the floor, or nearby table. It becomes vulnerable to being stolen. The dog's attention is now divided between you and their reinforcer.

Where possible be variable about your reserve location and in the case of anxious dogs keep all the treats and toys on you.

Once you begin to see how the reinforcers in these examples affect the behaviours, you begin to realise that the dog is only a respondent in the pool of reinforcer "currents". They, and we, find resistance to reinforcement patterns almost impossible.

3. TIMING

Clicker training is invaluable at teaching you observation skills, co-ordination and analysis of behaviour. You have to understand what you want to click, what is likely to stimulate the behaviour, and be able to anticipate the behaviour so that you can mark with precision. Teaching behaviours with clicker training fine tunes your skills, but you mostly work in small pockets of micro behaviours.

Many times we inadvertently reinforce unwanted behaviours throughout the day and during all interaction with the dog. The timing of these reinforcers, although seemingly small, can contribute more than you appreciate.

The main question is how to ensure that the reinforcer has been paired to the behaviour by the dog. The puppy that has sat because a person approached, with open, clear body language intent on greeting. But paused after the pup sat to talk to the owner. Four seconds have now passed between the sit, clever puppy, and the reinforcer: attention, touch, focus. This is dangerous territory.

The time gap can only be measured by the continuing success of the repetition of the wanted behaviour.

I have enjoyed life with dogs at both extremes of the "memory access" scale. Kent, delightful Gordon, is a "slow memory access" kinda boy. He sits, ponders the sit, and then looks for the outcome. As a puppy he would sit, and wait a good 10 seconds before thinking of something else to do. Flink, fast, keen, easily motivated and distracted collie, will hold a sit for micro seconds before moving onto the next behaviour. With Kent, you could say hello, make a long distance call, then reinforce with success. With Flink, you get the sit, take a deep breath and begin to bend over too slowly and she's off onto more exciting behaviours: washing your face.

As each dog will have a connecting limit between the behaviour and the reinforcer, so will different behaviours. Kent enjoys sitting back, letting the world arrive, so for him the sit is a patient type of behaviour, Flink is designed for action, and sitting is definitely not in her vision as a "suitable behaviour for a sheepdog". It takes us back to the added reinforcement coming from choice, which behaviours these dog choose to do, and their individual, instinctive preferences.

Counter preference behaviours need closer reinforcers, than preferential behaviours, their tolerance for a gap between the behaviour and its outcome is more flexible.

EXAMPLE: PAW WAVE

Mabel is now 12 years old and one of her first behaviours with clicker training as a 3 month old pup was a paw wave. Her choice is her right paw. This may be because I taught the behaviour when sitting on the floor facing her, and I am left handed, using my preference for that hand as a cue. Or the effect of first learning, or she is simply right handed. 11 years later, after teaching both behaviours to verbal cues, hand cues and objects, her left paw still had lower tolerance of the gap between the marker and the reinforcer. Even without a marker, the right paw stays strong, the left is the first to fade. The reinforcement history of that right paw can be counted not just in quantity of food delivered: read 2500 here, but also reinforcement from this being her first learning moment (deeply emotional event—"What, I can make Her click?"), and her preferential paw. All contributors to reinforcing the right paw over the left paw.

EXERCISE

If you have two behaviours that can happen out of the same behaviour see if your change in your timing is more tolerant on one than the other:

The dog can begin in the sit and be cued to stand or down.

The dog can be standing in front and cued to spin clockwise or anti-clockwise.

Begin with marking both behaviours when correct, and see if, by increasing the time delay to the delivery of the reinforcer whether one behaviour deteriorates sooner than the other.

Time delayed reinforcers are not advisable as a training strategy, but useful as an exercise in measuring preferences. But delayed reinforcers, where you move through a predictable pattern of behaviour that always end in a reinforcer, is a great training strategy and should be used frequently.

Mark the behaviour, but then begin a pattern of showing surprise and how deeply impressed you are, reach into you pocket, chat to the dog, rummage with your food container, take your time to select a treat, keep your focus on the dog, and you can delay the delivery of the reinforcer for 30 seconds. The whole PATTERN is the reinforcer through the predictable outcome and the subtle reinforcers of focus, your reactions and clear intentions.

At the other extreme, mark the behaviour and avoid movement, or eye contact for 5 seconds and the dog will begin to mentally sink. This is not often intentional, but I see it far too frequently, when the trainer has clicked, but then been distracted by something, and delayed delivery. A new behaviour will rarely tolerate this punishing strategy.

If you need to reinforce a behaviour but are without the effective tools, begin the pattern whilst you run to the toy box or fridge, or borrow what is needed. An excellent strategy to use for competition where reinforcers are limited.

4. SPEED AND PACE

This subtle reinforcer plays a large part in influencing the behaviour. Bringing mimic, management and arousal into the behaviour cycle, adds reinforcement.

I usually teach my dogs free shaping whilst sitting in a chair—it makes for easier viewing of the whole dog, it serves as a clear environmental cue.

I have always considered that the absence of information, no click, is very ambiguous. Should the dog try a different behaviour, try the same behaviour with more intensity, or wait for a cue? Once a behaviour has been taught and put "on cue" it should not occur unless cued. Sure, dogs sit on many frequent occasions throughout their day without cues from me, but when training I do not want my dogs anticipating, or spinning when cued to back up, or taking a bow when cued to jump. Free shaping requires the dog to experiment with behaviours and it is very likely that the dog will try a behaviour that is on-cue, since that behaviour will have a long reinforcement history to have got to the point to go on-cue. Therefore I need to discriminate when these trained behaviours can be freely tried and experimented with, so I sit in a chair to unlock the cue management of taught behaviours.

Out of this protocol Speck self taught a new behaviour of trying the down with no luck, and then backing up, no luck. His next offering was a backing up in the down! Made me laugh and it is fast becoming a signature trick. I would not have thought to ask him for that, it was his suggestion.

In free-shaping the dog is able to choose and puzzle solve and responding to cues is irrelevant. I sit with quiet body language and try to mimic the atmosphere the dog creates. Kent the Gordon, whose planet revolves a little slowly can get flustered and loose confidence if I follow the same pace and pattern of the collies. He tests out a behaviour, listens for the click, and then looks for the food. This can take 3–5 seconds. I make sure I never throw the food until he looks at me to see where it is going. Although a clicker puppy, the brain path between click and food needs to be remembered on each occasion. For him, fast feeding or flurries of action distract him and he takes time to get back into the difficult task of concentrating.

At the other extreme I have students with very fast thinking dogs, who probably exceed the thinking rate of their trainer. Some dogs have an exceedingly fast planet and must regard us a slow motion creatures. What often happens with these out of sync rhythms, is the person tries to speed up to the pace of the dog. This is never successful. The pace and speed should always match the rate of the slowest participant. Can you add several figures faster than your norm? Perhaps with many hundreds of hours practice the speed would increase naturally, but imagine what it feels like to try and make your brain compute maths formula quicker—you would just lose it.

All dogs can learn to wait for the Slow People syndrome. In fact it is essential, since their behaviour often happens so fast you have no chance to anticipate when to click. You can see the dogs glance at you to check that you are watching and then in slow motion press their paw on the object. The bright ones have also learned to cue the Slow Person to press the clicker....

Usually the strategy will need to match the pace of the behaviour. If you are teaching calm, relaxed behaviours deliver the food with calmness. If you are teaching quick responsive, energetic behaviours then add action to the delivery. You can toss the treat for a catch, throw it across the room for a race, bounce it off the walls for fun. This combination of action and food allows you to combine the instinctive behaviours of chase, kill with the beneficial high frequency of food, with only a moderate drain on the energy. To teach the same behaviours for a chasing for the toy game can be limited by early onset of exhaustion.

The sit is a good example of a behaviour with two parts: doing the sit, is fast, smart, responsive, but maintaining the sit is poised and controlled. When teaching a dog the action of sitting, active food is ideal for repetitive practice.

If I set the dog up for a sit or down for duration, I will calmly deliver the treat to the dog. If I set up the sit or down for a recall, then the treat is thrown. I maintain these patterns with the different behaviours, which each have their own set-up cue, to influence the energy level of the behaviour. The sit for duration will have some relaxation in the joints and the sit for recall will be tense and poised for immediate flight—as is the sit prior to heel set off, sit prior to retrieve or start lines. Get this around the wrong way and the dog can fidget during a stay exercise or be slow to move out of the sit for the following activities.

5. REINFORCING SPECIFIC BEHAVIOUR TO INDUCE ANTICIPATION

As the location where the reinforcer is delivered pulls at the behaviour so does the behaviour during the reinforcement. Duration behaviours need to have their reinforcer delivered in situ, if the dog begins to get stressed, or tense, the reinforcement history in that behaviour may support the dog through the moment.

I used to compete in obedience with a highly sensitive dog that was always anxious about the punishing behaviour of other handlers, particularly at the completion of the stay exercise. On return I would kneel down to join him in the down position, encourage the roll over and spend 15–20 seconds on a very indulgent belly rub. I would always be vigilant in protecting him from the interference from others dogs releasing from the exercise, and usually stay in position whilst the other handlers left the ring. If he became anxious, I could see him starting to anticipate the belly rub, and emotionally that possibly calmed him, or else he was trying to cue me to return as quickly as possible! But if the dog anticipates a highly arousing joyous behaviour on completion you can begin to see how this conflicts with the duration exercise. These two behaviours become chained together and when paired frequently both affect each other.

I build several two-behaviour chains and deliberately focus the reinforcer on the second behaviour to "draw" the first behaviour to that outcome. When teaching a spin, I want my dogs to return to the position they started in, which is either the stand in front or the stand in heel position. They are taught with a target stick, the action of turning will be clicked, shaped by the target, but the position of standing in front, quite still, will be the behaviour that attracts the reinforcer. By glueing these two behaviours together the dog will always try to get to that second behaviour when the first behaviour is cued.

To achieve the second behaviours in this mini chain, do not be afraid to lure after the click. I am teaching the puppy to go from the stand position to the drop position, the click marks the successful behaviour but the food is used to lure him back to a standing position. This has two advantages: firstly to prevent the hip settle in the drop position, and secondly to draw him to a clean "lift" action. His muscles control the drop but stay ready for the lift action.

When teaching loose lead walking, I will expect the dog to maintain a position relative to me. This is where the reinforcer, which may be food or focus and attention is delivered. The lead may be loose when the dog is four feet in front of me, but this is NOT the place I want the dog to maintain.

The click is most effective in allowing us to separate the behaviour that earns the reinforcer, from the location or behaviour in which the reinforcer is delivered. Getting your head out the rabbit hole is a clickable event, returning to me for a tug game is the location of the behaviour that enjoys the reinforcement action.

I have seen agility dogs unable to maintain forward momentum or changes of direction when the reinforcer is always in close proximity to the handler. The mark of success, either a click or a shout will draw the dog to the handler for the reinforcer. This may be advantageous when training a dog that is likely to depart, but over zealous application can be recognised by the agility somersault—where the handler goes tip-over-ass as they try to avoid the dog.

This anticipation of specific behaviour in specific locations can teach:

RETRIEVE: DESIRE TO RETURN WITH THE OBJECT

Begin with establishing a toy as the link in a terrific tug game, over several weeks this toy is only used for this activity. It is not allowed to be used for self rewarding games or with other dogs. Once the dog recognises the toy and launches into the tug without prompting, toss the tug to the floor about 6–10 feet away. As the dog runs to the toy, remain silent (very, very rarely will a dog not run after a moving object, it is an instinctive, self reinforcing behaviour), as the dog picks up the item, remain silent, as the dog looks at you react with focus, attention and immensely impressive drama.

React with encouragement when the dog runs out, you can reinforce disengagement, and the dog can take off after arriving at the toy. After all, you have reinforced running off from you. Reinforce when the dog takes hold of the toy or picks it up, and the dog can now take off running away from you with the toy. Be precise with your timing so that the combination of picking up AND looking at you (you may presume that what the dog is looking at is what they are thinking about) is reinforcement by your animation, and the reinforcement history of the tug-and-you combination will draw the dog back to you. The reinforcer? ..... well more tug! That long and high enjoyable history of the tug and you together will make returning to you with the tug act like a magnet.

If the dog is not predisposed to enjoy tug, then associate the toy with their favourite activity. The Gordons are soft mouthed and tug training is not their preference. As most gundogs their joy is being able to hold a very large, mouthful or something soft and furry, for several minutes. When planning retrieve training, I spend many hours lushing over that very special Gordon holding that quite magnificent teddy bear. Even hesitating to draw breath stimulates them to move closer. But for the dogs that truly enjoy the hold, removal of the toy can be punishing. If every time they arrive within hand reach, you relieve them of their instinctive pleasure then begin to wonder why they would repeat the behaviour of returning to you? Reinforce arrival with several seconds of drama and amazement, and then ask them to swap what they have for something of equal pleasure—another toy, or in the case of most gundogs, a chunk of meat!

WEAVE TRAINING: MAINTAINING FORWARD MOMENTUM

Even if you free shape the behaviour, planning to deliver the treat at the final point of the behaviours will draw the dog to that point. You can place your box of treats at the end of the chute or run, click for a great entry behaviour, then proceed to that location to deliver the treat. Back chaining from this point will ensure that first behaviour is attracted to second behaviour. But if your dog has a long reinforcement history of coming to you when they hear the click, then do not be surprised if the dog leaves the behaviours as soon as they hear the click.

RESPONSE ON THE MARKER

I have seen many thousands of dogs and a few hundred of other species clicker trained. It is fascinating to see the different styles, which generally group geographically or within different activities, of using the click. I have seen dogs stop all action when they hear the click (food delivered *in situ*) and I have seen dogs pop out of the behaviour to stand in front of the handler on click and I have seen dogs complete the behaviour and move onto a reinforcement station. These different reactions evolve from different teaching styles.

All styles are appropriate in different situations. Some behaviours are best complimented by *in situ* reinforcement, some by At The Station reinforcement. But use of the wrong strategy can unbalance the behaviour and make it so much harder for the dog to learn. I think they have enough challenges trying to understand us, it becomes our responsibility to make it as consistent, clear and effective as possible.

There is nothing to stop you using a different marker sound for each response. Even the standard box clicker can give two quite different sounds by changing the angle of your thumb. Place the smallest surface area, the tip, onto the end of the metal and the click will be a loud, sharp sound, flatten your thumb and make the greatest surface area cover the metal and the dimple, and the sound will be dull. One for action, catch the hotdog response, the other will be remain in position response, lunch will be served to you.

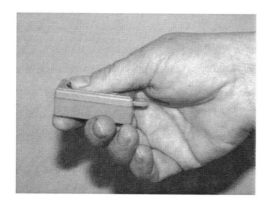
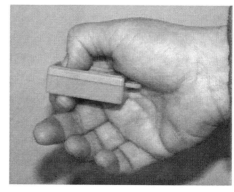

left: the soft click,
right: the loud click

6. HOW MUCH? MEASURING THE VALUE OF THE REINFORCER

This question is rather similar to the novice query: "Have I always got to carry food with me?" Well, yes, if you are trying to maintain a behaviour that is counter instinctive. Leaving an escaping rabbit to return to you for some average woodland browsing is certainly not an instinctive behaviour. But many thousands of reinforcer for returning to you when in a non-aroused state, may give you some chance to getting the call off when chasing prey. Alternatively you will need a reinforcer of equal, or greater, value as chasing prey—and that would be chasing prey alongside you, their pack. I personally don't carry spare rabbits under my coat for those occasions, but when the opportunity arises I recall the Gordons to search ground that I have seen pheasants on.

The value of the reinforcer can only be measured by the occurrence of the behaviour, maintaining strength or repeating more frequently. If your dog will return for hot dog when woodland browsing, then a hot dog is more value that woodland browsing. But more likely this success is down to the knowledge that after returning for the food treat, the dog will also go back to woodland browsing. The recall return is a temporary break. If your call to return is food treat AND end of the browsing, then the punisher of ending the browsing will become greater than the treat, and your call to return will fade. You can begin good habits in young dogs before the browsing hunting behaviour has a long history of reinforcement. As youngsters running through woods or field is inter- esting and the more it is practised, the more it is reinforced until it exceeds all other reinforcers in value. Kent was a great recall Gordon, which is somewhat of a contradiction, until around 3 years old. (Well I said his planet turns slowly). I became lax between 2 and 3 years old in reinforcing the return, in the meantime the hunting thrill was gaining strength.

To maintain a good recall when out on a walk, practise frequent returns for high value reinforcers, such as great treats, and only end the walk when the dog has experienced enough satisfying browsing. The final recall, when the walk ends may need an extra reinforcer, such as some rub down to clean off, or a good drink of water, or a new area to explore on lead with you. This strategy is great for dogs that enjoy browsing. My collies enjoy being sheepdogs and use each other to "work" or practise their herding skills whilst out in the field. They can easily have as much entertainment and reinforcement if the environment was a car park. The centre of the herding is me, and for these type of dogs getting them to go off and browse is almost impossible. I would only recall, which can be tricky since they want to outrun and flank, at the end of the walk and the key dog needs to be removed to release the others from their tasks. Once he breaks his "eye" and begins to browse and mark, then the others will mimic. I can anticipate this behaviour as we turn towards home, and put it on cue: "That'll do."

The value of the reinforcer can only be measured by the behaviour, at that time, in that environment.

ANTICIPATION AND DISAPPOINTMENT

There is no evidence that a larger piece of food is a higher value reinforcer. In fact large pieces of food, or difficult to chew pieces of food, can be lower value reinforcers since the tummies fill quicker, and in the case of Gordons, they forget what they were doing whilst chewing: "in the food zone".

The higher value can only be measured because:

   1. The behaviour will be repeated at a high quality level, more intense from the arousal triggered by anticipating a more interesting treat.

   2. Will repeat more often or for more duration for a single reinforcer.

   3. Is strong in a more difficult environment, in anticipation of the high value treat.

You can only get the best from high value reinforcers in tandem with anticipation. If your dog is used to brown rice as a treat, but only you know you have some cooked heart ready to go, then the dog will respond with a "brown rice" type of behaviour. If you let the dog take a whiff of the treat bag containing heart, then their level of arousal will shoot up, and you will see a change in the behaviour:

   The focus on you for a cue

   The response to the cue

   The intensity, or quality

You will get more bananas for your pound, more bang for your buck.

Anticipation seems to be reinforcing in itself. When you have an event to look forward to several months ahead, such as a holiday, there is as much fun in the anticipation of this as there is in the event itself. In fact sometimes the event can be a disappointment if we have let our anticipatory imagination run wild. We cannot know how the dogs anticipate, if they do at all. We can only see the evidence of a more aroused and intense state when the reinforcer is clearly stated and of high value. This is not luring or bribery, just good communication. There may also be some element of the chemical soup originated from this arousal state becoming slightly addictive. Do you enjoy the "buzz" of anticipation? Anticipation arousal is a very workable state, and more useful than excitement arousal from a high energy game, since there is focus on earning the reinforcer. This will come from your teaching style, where reinforcers are paired with effort. If my dogs view their reinforcer their first question is not "I want that", but "What can I do for that?"

The flip side of anticipation is the disappointment when a piece of heart is anticipated, but a piece of brown rice is delivered. I notice I can get away with this maybe two or three times, but once the dog seems to register only brown rice is on offer, the behaviour begins to fade. In fact some dogs simply refuse the lower value treat, and in these cases you have to play honest—only pay the high value. If the treat is important enough to them to refuse, then you do not want that attitude paired with training.

The fading is not usually an immediate "shan't" attitude since the chemicals of anticipation are floating around the dog's system, but the intensity begins to fade, as does the response. Ideally if those high level treats are not suitable for continual use, you intersperse them with brown rice but on a schedule that maintains the quality of the behaviour. Somewhere between 3:1, or 4:1, 4 pieces of rice to 1 piece of heart, but you must take the evidence of sufficient heart to rice from the quality of the behaviours the dog is demonstrating.

IT IS THE NATURE OF BEHAVIOUR TO CHANGE

And nature does not make is easy for us.

I have taught my puppy to sit for a piece of cooked chicken. A cube about half the size of my thumbnail. Once my puppy has repeated this behaviour 4–500 times I will reduce the value of the reinforcer. The sit has become much easier to achieve, is it more of a reflex than a considered response, and the puppy, now 7 months old, will get reaction, affection or attention as a reinforcer for a plain sit, but it will always get some reinforcer. If I continue to feed the cube of chicken, I will be de-valuing it since the behaviour that requires that value has become easier to do. The sit will still get good quality reinforcement, but not as the same high value.

Imagine a cube of cooked chicken is the value of 1 unit. To earn this the pup has to focus, respond with self control to the lure, or remember what they have to do to get that treat. This is quite an achievement for this 10 week old pup, who is high energy and easily aroused. I set the value of this combined effort as 1 unit of effort.

As time and repetition increases the sit competency the pup will need less skill, concentration and memory skills to earn the same value reinforcer—1 unit. I may be using these treats for shaping exercises, teaching a new behaviour or recognition of self control, but by over paying for the competent sit, I risk de-valueing the 1 unit reinforcer, and may affect the amount of effort put into more complex behaviours that only earn the same reinforcement.

But in more difficult situations, perhaps a sit before the dog leaves the car, I will revert to 1 unit of reinforcement, since the amount of effort required to achieve that behaviour will be far higher than the sit in my kitchen.

It is highly unlikely that you will have the time to measure the reinforcer on every occasion. But remember to recognise when the effort is greatly in excess of the standard 1 unit reinforcer and use sufficient reinforcers to match the effort required to perform the behaviour. My Gordons will respond to recall for food when in the garden, but not when in the field. The food value has completely changed and I would require to compete with the highest reinforcer: bird hunting. I have a secret weapon for high value reinforcement with the Gordons and that is intense focus and loud adoration, drama, body rubs for at least 60 seconds. This is quite exhausting, but definitely high value for their temperament. My collies would be appalled at such a display of adoration. A simple "cool", is all they require. Job done.

One technique that worries me is the strategy of using too much of "yourself" as part of a standard unit of reinforcement. When clicker training a new behaviour, the dog learns to memorise what they are doing at the time of the mark and seek their reward. This is a highly cognitive process and needs plenty of relaxed concentration. If, when you deliver the food treat, you simulta-neously add several murmurs, or even dramas of amazement and approval you can disrupt the concentration. The dog needs to be able to learn without trying to seek approval or an emotional response from you at the same time. In this situation let the clicker and food do the talking and reserve your valuable approval for those times when there is a genuine increase in effort or you are · without external reinforcement. You may need to plan to associate sounds such as "good boy" with the delivery of food, but be aware of over using it unnec-essarily. The amount you need is the amount that is sufficient to strengthen, or increase frequency of the behaviour.

You can vary the value of the reinforcer in an unpredictable way, with variable reinforcement. *Note: NOT variable schedule of reinforcement, this is when the same reinforcer is delivered on a variable schedule, ie 1st, 3rd, 8th, 13th repetition etc.* For this sit I will give you attention, for the next sit I will put the lead on to go for a walk, for the next sit I will give a food treat, but there is always reinforcement. This variability will only work if at a regular intervals the dog has received an exceedingly high value, important reinforcer, such as going for a walk. But if the dog only ever receives a pat on the head or a smile for a sit, then you can expect to get the same quality behaviour in return. The predictability of a high reinforcer elicits strong behaviour, the predictability of a poor reinforcer will elicit a weak behaviour.

Those important, must have, behaviours such as a recall, should always predict the best quality reinforcer to maintain the quality of the behaviour. It is too important for you to get slack on.

STEPPING DOWN THE QUANTITY OF REINFORCEMENT

This is a process that must be handled with care. Reducing the reinforcer value before the behaviour is fixed in quality can have the effect of lowering the quality of the behaviour or response to the cue.

I train my dogs for competition conditions that do not allow food or toys during the performance. In the junior classes they would be required to demonstrate approximately 20 behaviours in 60 seconds, and I can plan for a final reinforcement of exceedingly high value once outside the ring. You can train a routine in a back chain, where each behaviour cues the subsequent behaviour which ends in highest value reinforcement. An exercise such as retrieve, containing a handful of behaviours is ideal for this technique. The final behaviour, which is the Give, is reinforced with a 10 unit highest value: for the collies another chase and capture, for the Gordons several pieces of food, with 30 seconds of adoration. I have taken the Gordon Unit of a 10 to a 12, with several people simultaneously demonstrating adoration. You begin to train the chain by teaching each behaviour, in any order, for the standard 1 unit reinforcer:

Marking the thrown article = 1 standard unit reinforcer

Maintaining focus on the article = 1 standard unit reinforcer

Maintaining the sit position to heel = 1 standard unit reinforcer

Going out with focus and purpose on a single cue = 1 standard unit reinforcer

Planning the clean pick up = 1 standard unit reinforcer

Turning back to focus on you = 1 standard unit reinforcer

Running with the article = 1 standard unit reinforcer

Preparing to collect into a sit = 1 standard unit reinforcer

Maintaining the present until the cue to give. = 1 standard unit reinforcer

Then you back chain the behaviours together in clusters, highly reinforcing the last behaviour.

CLUSTER 1

Maintaining the position = 5 unit reinforcer

Maintaining focus on the article + Maintaining the position = 5 unit reinforcer

Marking the thrown article + Maintaining focus on the article + Maintaining the position = 5 unit reinforcer

CLUSTER 2

Turning back to focus on you = 5 unit reinforcer

Going out with focus and purpose on a single cue + Turning back to focus on you = 5 unit reinforcer

Planning the clean pick up + Going out with focus and purpose on a single cue + Turning back to focus on you = 5 unit reinforcer

CLUSTER 3

Maintaining the present until the cue to give = 5 unit reinforcer

Running with the article + Maintaining the present until the cue to give = 5 unit reinforcer

Preparing to collect into a sit + Running with the article + Maintaining the present until the cue to give = 5 unit reinforcer

As competency is achieved in each cluster, which is probably in the region of 3–400 repetitions, you can reduce the reinforcer down to a 1 standard unit.

Next the three clusters are back chained together:

Cluster 3—return and present

Cluster 2—run out and pick up

Cluster 1—control during throw

This complete chain is primarily reinforced with a 10 unit reinforcer until high level competency is guaranteed and then the reinforcer can be reduced in value.

By increasing the value of the final behaviour in the clusters, or when the clusters are chained, it begins to drive anticipation towards that end reinforcer. These chains will only work when they are always predictable, so that anticipation can be used to its best advantage.

This technique is very effective is chains of 3–4 behaviours, but when performing 4 times that number of behaviours, anticipating of the next behaviour is a real problem, especially when there is a music cue the dog can recognise, or when some behaviours get a strongly reinforcing response from the audience.

In this situation I teach each behaviour for a standard 1 unit. After several hundred repetitions the behaviour is very fixed. 600 repetitions of a behaviour, such as a spin, practised in batches of 20, would only take 30 training sessions. My criteria to reduce the reinforcer value:

1. The behaviour is without variation in normal or average training conditions. That is, in a location where the dog has a history of a high reinforcement, with minimal distractions.

2. The behaviour always happens when cued

3. The behaviour does not happen unless cued, it is not triggered by the toy or my posture or choreography.

If these criteria are not in place the reduction of the value of the reinforcer, or requiring two behaviours for 1 standard unit will diminish the behaviours and leave you with a variable quality.

I will then link this quality-fixed behaviour to another that has already been through the repetition pattern and meets the requirements. I keep notes of my "bank" of fixed behaviours, and behaviours that are:

Work in Progress: Learning

and

Work in Progress: Repetition, Fluency.

This new behaviour will then become part of collections of two, three or four or eight from this bank. Each individually successful behaviour will get a minor reinforcer: perhaps a smile, attention, or "cool" or extra animation. Once the collection is completed there will be a high reinforcer of value 10—probably a great game with a toy for half a minute. This strategy of collecting behaviours together is always reinforced at the (variable) end with the highest level of reinforcer.

As the dogs become experienced and anticipate that final reinforcer you can see collections of many behaviours with full strength and obviously reinforced. But individually there is hardly any noticeable reinforcer. By this stage being allowed to continue the chain becomes reinforcing, taking the dog closer to the final jamboree.

We tend to use a term to describe when a behaviour has a such as strong repetition history, for example 3000 reinforcers, that it is "self-reinforcing"; ie; the behaviour has been paired with so much reinforcement that is has become a secondary reinforcer. This is certainly true of most learned behaviours, but for behaviours contrary to instinctive behaviour, they can never become self reinforcing. That instinctive behaviour will always pull at the contrary behaviour. The only way to measure that a behaviour has become a secondary reinforcer is to shape a new behaviour with the cue for as a marker. (See Chapter 5)

STEPPING UP THE VALUE OF THE REINFORCEMENT

Larger pieces of food do not usually result in a demonstrable increase in the quality or frequency of the behaviour. The more food the dog has over a sessions the quicker the stomach fills, and the digestive process can begin to make the dog, especially puppies, sleepy.

There are occasions when we need to increase the reinforcement value because the dog has completed the behaviour with extra panache, or under pressure of a strongly distracting cue, or in a new environment without a reinforcement history. The value needs to be maintained at that level whilst the effort continues. It is so risky to feed just one "jackpot" and then reduce on the next repetition.

TO INCREASE FOOD REINFORCER:

Repeat the delivery of one piece of very small treat several times, at the rate of one every second. Perhaps include some joint searching or catching or activity such as chasing. But allow for the added value to impact on the subsequent behaviour with a break in focus or the opposite effect of an increase in arousal.

TO INCREASE ATTENTION:

I use a look, of the gentle kind, when the group of dogs are around. I may be looking at Speck, but suddenly Quick throws in the sit, somewhat late, but an achievement for that youngster. My attention will switch from Speck to Quick, both will probably get additional reinforcement of a treat, but that "look" marked Quick's thinking, and for less important moments a short period of attention is an immediate and important reinforcer.

You can increase this value by moving towards the dog, adding your total focus, or placing yourself at eye level to the dog and having a conversation. This can then increase with touching, provided that dog is reinforced by it, until you get up to the Gordon Adoration Sequence.

Duration in any of these stages will increase the value. See how tiring it is to give 60 seconds of adoration—and see the consequences! It seems a very long minute, but, wow, one minute of investment that has diamond value. *Note: hold onto dogs that become aroused by this sequence, I have had more than one fat lip from the Gordon explaining how much he adores me as well.*

TO INCREASE CONNECTION:

This is not usually a reinforcer for training, but a great reinforcer for relaxation and general appreciation of each other's company and consideration. My staircase is a wonderful connection spot. It allows us to sit side by side, probably at eye level, and choose to touch or not. But just a sit down for 60 seconds and chat to the dog about how their Tuesday is progressing is valuable to your dog. A walk MAY be connecting, but most likely minimal since the dog's focus will be outwards and searching. One little rescue soul that was far too humble was greatly built in self-confidence by being my front seat passenger for several weeks. Yes, she wore a seat belt. But as I ran errands, to and fro college classes with the occasional visit to a new lay-by, we would chat, share lunch and have only each other for company. Great stuff, I enjoyed it, it was her special task.

TO INCREASE POWER:

This is a wonderfully easy and effective way to reinforce when no toys or treats are handy. My 10 week old pup is hanging out in the kitchen, everything that is happening is quite a distance above his head. He sits. Wow, that stops me, and I come down to his level with lots of attention and touching (to prevent the jumping). "OK", he thinks, "I can get Her to me by doing ..... errrr..... Hey? A sit? Yep, down she comes again. This IS cool".

Sometimes the dogs will move onto their beds without prompting, after a minute's settle, I go over and give them some attention—of their choice, but mostly is of the upside down variety.

Teaching that pup to return with the toy, you stand quite quietly until the pup looks at you whilst holding the toy and then you begin to animate. Wow, they have the power to turn you from a statue staring off into space, to a very interesting, attractive person with a magnetic personality. This is a great technique to get the youngster to think about you when out browsing, or teach the beginnings of a recall. It would be unusual for a dog to go for a free walk, or cruise around their garden or field, without glancing at you. If you are standing there yacking away to a friend, or on the phone then you relieve them of the need to check where you are. The same with continually saying the their name or calling them to catch up. Make like a tree, and they will give you glancing check-in looks. You can reinforce those looks by responding with a mirroring look and verbal response: "Hi, how's it going?" The dog may not travel over to you for further interaction, but you will definitely notice an increase in this behaviour by just a minor animation, or even turning towards the dog and following them a few steps.

Once this behaviour is frequent you can begin to think of increasing magnetic animation with pocket searching, flourishing a toy for play, or running after a thrown toy. These would attract the dog to run towards you, and you can then choose how to reinforce that behaviour with connection, play, attention, or just simply begin the Woodlands Dog Walker's Dance. If you want to decrease the dog's connection to you during free running, ignore their looks at you, ignore them when they stand in front of you, as they focus on something else just follow them mindlessly. Add to this your responsibility to pick up their poo and you can begin to see that the classical "going for a walk with the dog" can slip into: Dog Goes Browsing and Marking Territory, whilst the carer (you) chauffeurs them to the hunting area, drags along behind, cleans them up and chauffeurs them home again. No wonder some dogs develop the attitude of a super-hormonal 15 year old teenager.

TO INCREASE PLAY VALUE:

Most games come with different intensity depending on the dog's particular instinctive skills. For a dog that enjoys tugging you can increase the value with a brain-shaking session, for the dog that enjoys stalking and capture, the time duration of the stalking can increase. For the dogs that enjoy carrying, add animation during the carrying, joint running and jumping together.

You need to increase the value of play to reinforce the behaviours of play. When teaching a dog to tug, it is essential they take a healthy grip. This includes a bite using most of their teeth, so that the muscle strength in the jaw is evenly distributed. The gundogs have a gentle grip, and large objects are easier for them so that the jaw can displace the power of the grip on all the teeth. Some dogs can grip with just their front teeth, and occasionally this is fine, but not as a long term strategy. Always select objects that allow for 60% of the mouth to be employed and is also easy for your hands to hold.

Some of the best, or safest, tugs are designed with a central area for the dog to grip, beginning with the gentle textures for puppies and soft mouthed adults, right up to the sacking fibre for professional grippers. At least one end, but preferably both, should have a loop handle to slip your hand into. It is far easier to take a grip on a handle around your wrist, that just gripping with your fingers. A clear delineation between your part of the tug and the dog's part helps with the dogs that consider all the tug is theirs. Remember that *you* will need some reinforcement from this process and pulled back muscles do not contribute to reinforcement.

When teaching tug there are some behaviours you want to reinforce, and others that you wish to punish. The constant reinforcement is the continuation of joint tugging (shared kill), your focus and attention and using an instinctive behaviour. You can quickly shape out unwanted behaviours such as biting the tug close to your hands. You can see the dog re-grip closer and closer as a competitive threat to your hold, and as soon as that begins, drop the toy and take your focus elsewhere. Drop the toy but keep your focus on the dog will reinforce this threat strategy. Go talk to a tree, do not watch the dog, go sit in the car. Leave for about three minutes and then reappear and offer a game with the No 2 Tug. Do not try this strategy if you do not have a reserve tug toy. You must also punish the dog placing their feet against you for extra leverage. Our legs were never designed for this interaction, again, leave, walk away. Just getting the toy is less reinforcing than playing with you, especially if you reappear with something much better that includes the highly arousing game.

Behaviour you want to increase, such as taking the clean grip on the first attempt, can easily be shaped during the game. A clicker is most essential with the speed of these aroused behaviours, offer the toy to the dog, click for the clean grip and go on to begin the play. I calculate 1 standard of unit of tug as: stationary, noisy (verbally from me) and lasting only 3 seconds.

Reinforce maintaining the grip: if the dog slackens their mouth and loses grip, you MUST take the tug away and enjoy it, by yourself, for 3 seconds. If the dog lets go before cued, and you offer it back straight away, why would the dog continue to hold? If they are maintaining the grip, reinforce with a double unit, 6 seconds of tug, or let the dog pull backwards and you begin to inch forward.

For shy grippers and tuggers make a tug at least 6 foot long, (2m) and only play when you are at this length. Tie string to the tug toy, make sure you have a good handle, and you will find that the distance from you increases confidence to tug. (See Learning About Dogs: *Whippits* DVD training for using this arousal to teach self control).

Reinforce the release with a re-start of the game. Bring the dog close to you, take hold of their collar under their chin in an underarm grip and hold tight enough to prevent any further tugging. As the dog's jaw begins to slacken, which you can feel with the tension on the tug, click, and resume tugging. Even for the King Grip Merchants, once the tugging tension has stopped, they will begin to slightly relax, not let go, but relax. If you can reinforce this relaxation, you are on the way to achieve a great release—after all releasing and relinquishing is the ONLY was to get the game to start again.

---

7. REMOVING REINFORCEMENT

When all is excused and discussed, this is negative punishment. Is it effective, that is never in question, but if you are seeking to use reinforcers effectively this needs to be your last resort, not your first choice. Beware of personally getting reinforced by using this technique, it is often quick, and does not usually require lots of energy or effort, but it is often negligence or laziness that drives us to it.

Looking at it on a deeper level view the two choices: adding something pleasurable, and taking away something pleasurable. Which would you prefer? Not really a question is it.

There is a fall out when using the removal of something anticipated. Imagine a dog is stalking a rabbit, it has been hungry for several days and really needs that rabbit. If this one gets away, (loss of something desirable) is it going to try harder or just shrug and give up? In the case of extreme need, or instinctive behaviours, it is definitely going to try harder. In the case of learned behaviours you may well diminish the behaviour.

In the other world, the positive reinforcement sphere, there is a strengthened desire to earn, not to avoid. There is no fear of failure and trying unsuccessfully is just information. People and dogs that learn in that (natural) world are usually keen to learn more, remember what they have achieved and have a good relationship with the teacher, or teaching environment.

> If you eat all your vegetables I am going to let you watch TV for one hour, if you do not eat your vegetables I am going to send you straight to bed.

> If you sit at the door, I shall let you race into the garden, if you don't I shall push the door shut until you do as I say.

> If you stay at the start of the agility line up, I shall let you jump the jump, if you don't I shall put you on lead and take you out of the room.

I'm sure these options are not new to you, but if you ethically decide to stand in the world of positive reinforcement, then you must consider the alternatives, and check yourself when stepping into this negative punishment sphere.

I WANT MY CHILD TO LEARN TO EAT, AND ENJOY (THIS IS A KEY CONSIDERATION), VEGETABLES:

> I shall begin with asking the child to touch vegetables—reinforced with attention, social approval, play etc.

> Then I shall encourage the child to kiss vegetables, (using mirroring—adult kisses the bean, child kisses the bean)—reinforced with attention, social approval, play etc.

> Then I shall raise the bar and expect a bite, chew and swallow of one pea—reinforced with attention, social approval, play etc.

> And so on, until eating becomes a habit, not feared, and reinforcement reduces over the years.

Ideas courtesy of Tanya Byron, [cough] aka House of Tine Tearaways. This is a UK TV series—I have no experience in this field except a lasting requirement to re-shape my attitude to "enjoying" vegetables. I was a victim of deprivation of dessert as a child .... Aww.

I WANT MY DOG TO SIT AT A DOOR, WAIT UNDER CONTROL UNTIL I RELEASE THE DOG OR GO THROUGH FIRST AND CUE THE DOG TO FOLLOW.

This strategy is suitable for doors into new places, not the running out of the house doorway.

Begin with making the location a place with reinforcement history from you, not from the door.

Walk the dog up to the door begin to feed with treats for the focus to you.

Set the door up as open and repeat the same routine. If the dog can maintain focus on you in the open, inviting doorway, then the action of opening the door is irrelevant.

Repeat this until the dog has a sufficient history and responds to a cue to sit, or stand still.

Allow the dog to look through the door way and then reconnect to you, reinforce with food, or the cue to follow you through the door.

In Chapter 6 I will go through in detail how to re-balance a behaviour. You will need to be able to remove the reinforcement for the unwanted behaviour, and simultaneously you must begin a pattern of reinforcing the wanted behaviour. Negative punishment may inhibit the undesired behaviour but it does diddly-squat in teaching the dog what to do or how to behave. For the dog that scratches at the door to go out, have you TAUGHT it how to sit under control in that location?

---

8. SETTING UP A SECONDARY REINFORCER

For a marker or bridge to be effective it needs to be paired with a primary reinforcer. Most commonly used is the clicker and treats or whistle and fish, but other markers can be paired as well.

The marker needs to be consistent and be able to be delivered with precision and efficiency. You must identify in what circumstances and teaching situations you want to be able to use the marker. I do a lot, seriously a lot, perhaps 95%

of my teaching by free shaping. Some of the time the dog is working without watching me, they need to observe the object they are interacting with or they could be behind me or facing away. The clicker is an excellent, unambiguous tool for teaching, I am disciplined and do not move my hands when I click, making it an exclusively audible marker. I wait until the dog connects, facing me before delivering the food.

In dog training I have only seen a couple of trainers use a word as a marker with good effect. They had excellent discipline and used the word with consistent tone. What tends to happen in practice is the trainer uses the word, for instance "yes", but also animates as they say it: widen their eyes, nod their head, splay hands. This visual marker draws the dog to try to watch them all the time. This is a useful strategy, but with the limitations of compulsory visual contact.

Another marker is the cue to play, for instance: "get it". The dog drops to a down on cue, the handler give the marker "get it" which releases the dog from the behaviour to grab or chase the toy. Again this is usually accompanied with a physical signal.

All markers are built in the same way, you can either pair the marker simultaneously with the primary reinforcer, or in a chain where the primary follows the marker. As with any classical conditioning if the pairing is not maintained the effect will diminish.

One point you may want to consider is using different markers for different types of reinforcers. With using the verbal marker "get it" the dog is going to instantly arouse for the play, and strongly focus on you if you have the toy with you. At the other extreme you could pair the word "cool" with a slow stroke, and this would be effective when teaching a dog to relax, standing still for treatment or grooming, or as a reassurance that you are in control. I whistle as a marker for interaction, and this is particularly useful when I want to have a long extended marker

Having a range of markers allows you to enhance the emotional affect of the reinforcer if consistently paired.

9. MULTI REINFORCERS

Play is probably the best example of multiple reinforcers at work. It is one of the common behaviour of all young animals and is designed to enable learning—through skill development and acquisition of knowledge. Pups need to play with everything they need to learn about—their peers, different shaped dogs, cats in some cases, (I have even reared a pet lamb that "played" with the dogs) and especially you, in all your moods. I would even expect a pup to play with different skilled people so that they learned gentle games as well as appropriate rough games. The game can be anything that both parties enjoy, where it is beneficial to the long term development of both parties. We had a client with a skilled biting breed, developing towards a large biting breed. As a pup this youngster bit hard and it was painful for the person. The person resorted to wearing leather motor cycling gloves to protect his hands, and now the pup could enjoy the play with absolute freedom. Mmm, I probably don't need to spell out the long term result, but the dog's first instinct was to bite very hard, and only ever learned the gentle interaction when not aroused. Any game that took him to a certain level of arousal would result in that first learn: bite with all bullets firing.

During dog to dog play which in itself is highly reinforcing, the dog gets to learn and use many instinctive skills of not just how hard to bite, but where to bite for greatest effect, how not to get bitten in the important places, how to twist, use balance and leverage for best results. They learn where the "peace" zone is and how to trigger it, they learn how fast they need to be and the weaknesses of their opponents. There is constant interaction, arousal, and the added spice of "losing", playing The Game. The more games a dog plays the more skilled they become. If this tremendous package of reinforcement is only allowed once a week in the park or at puppy class, you can begin to see how nearly impossible it is for you to offer anything that tops the reinforcement. Why would a pup leave this reinforcing theatre to sit for a piece of dried cardboard (aka cheap treats)?

When playing with the pup or dog yourself you will need to set firm rules for what is allowed and what not, but what is left can still constitute one of the greatest games dogs can enjoy, and you also have opposable thumbs that allows you to throw balls. In addition to using instinctive skills, they have that continuous interaction, arousal, partnership, shared enjoyment, mutual learning and the added "frisson" of maybe this time they will win.

4 Building and Maintaining

This chapter will look at how you construct the behaviours you want and make a plan to keep those behaviours strong, resistant to change and a pleasure to enjoy. If you are looking to change an unwanted behaviour you will need to be able to construct the desired behaviour but also de-construct the unwanted behaviour. See Chapter 6 on "rebalancing behaviours".

Where possible, and some situations are impossible, the strategy for teaching is through errorless learning. We create a learning environment that stimulates the behaviour we are looking for, as close as possible to being error free. The foundation is laid down in high levels of reinforcement of the errorless behaviour and the reinforcers are gradually reduced as the dog improves in competency, understanding and skill. Some behaviours may need foundations that last ten times long than other behaviours, and some can begin a reducing reinforcement plan very soon. The practice is to slightly dip the reinforcers without trying to affect the behaviour. If there is a loss in quality return to the stimulus for the errorless and the high level reinforcement. If in doubt over pay, not under pay.

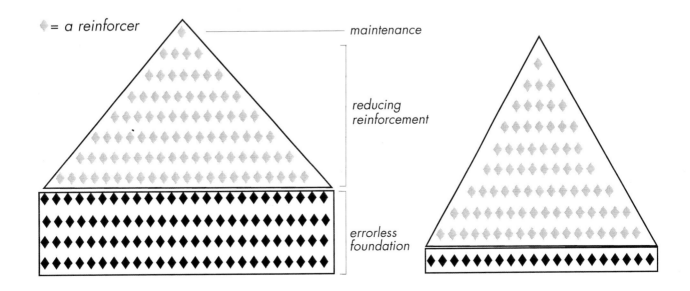

In time what is easily learned, such as the puppy walking by your side, or sitting at the door, can change as the pup grows and their priorities change. This will require you to alter the reinforcers to meet the needs of the behaviour. Sufficient reinforcement can only be measured by the maintenance, strengthening or frequency of the behaviour, never by what you "think" is sufficient, or the dog "ought" to find rewarding.

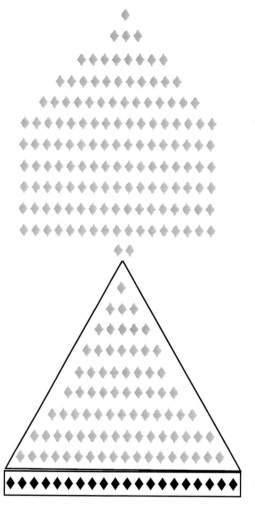

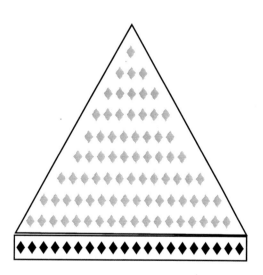

The behaviour taught initially, reinforcers reduced to a level to maintain the behaviour.

A change in the dog's environment or maturity requires a return to a high level of reinforcement to prevent the behaviour diminishing.

Behaviours are reliable to the ABC formula:

Antecedent: the cue, the stimulus, the trigger.

This can be external: a word from you, a sound to alert, a place of bad experiences, or internal: a full bladder, sleepiness, hunger etc.

Behaviour: the response, which is probably a cluster of behaviours:

moving your bottom onto the floor, whilst looking up and wagging your tail, a run to the window barking, sinking body language, a flattening of the ears, walking on egg shells, going to the garden searching for the right ground to eliminate, finding somewhere comfortable and secure, making a bed, going out hunting or trying to open the pantry door again.

Consequence: was it successful—reinforcement, was it unsuccessful—punishment.

When we build behaviours we need to have a clear idea what each of the A, B and C is going to be.

THE ANTECEDENT: initially we make use of several techniques as an antecedent, but in time change this to a cue from us.

> When house training a puppy we know they want to eliminate as soon as they wake, soon after eating, and after certain indicating behaviours: stopping playing, hunting around the floor. Although they can easily get caught short when involved in exciting activities, 90% of the time the indication of a full body is easy to predict. This is the current antecedent. Over time I will change this to a verbal cue, perhaps "hurry up, or be clean", and give this cue as I set the pup up at the place for elimination.

THE BEHAVIOUR: you need a clear idea of what you want. It is easier to teach in small bites than try to teach clusters of behaviours at the same time. The small bites can then be built into impressive collections.

Long term our aim is to get the pup to use a particular part of the garden as a toilet. As youngsters they are unable to alert you directly that their bodies are ready to pop, or may be unable to find their way to the correct door and may not remember where they have to use. We begin with recognising the signals, scoop up the pup, start to repeat our long term verbal cue, take the pup to the right spot, place them down, and when they eliminate, reinforce with a treat WHEN THEY ARE FINISHED. (Don't make the error of responding during elimination as this can result in only a partial completion and a trailing result.)

THE CONSEQUENCE: which reinforcer is going to be effective in this situation. Which is going to compliment the behaviour, which would not be appropriate and which is convenient. Have you prepared your reinforcers.

I prefer to use a treat for garden duties and keep some by the door so that I can grab and go without delay. If treatless I will give a fuss and attention. What I won't do is stuff the puppy outside the door and go back inside. Freezing cold or not.

One of the greatest challenges we face is finding that initial stimulus and protecting the error free opportunity. The dog cannot possibly understand verbal cues and they must only be introduced once the behaviour is well established, fluent and predictable on the initial antecedent. We then change the stimulus for several reasons:

◆ It enables us to call upon the behaviour in more than one place

◆ We can separate the initial antecedent from the behaviour

◆ It allows us to build chains and combine the small behaviours

Secondly we need to think ahead to the life of this behaviour. Where will I want it to occur, what are the likely environments, and how is it likely to change.

EXAMPLES

You may be lucky to share your life with a dog with a good understanding of some of these behaviours. But if you have read the previous chapter you should be "seeing with new eyes" and I would like you to read through and begin to understand how using the reinforcers with planning and care constructs strong and reliable behaviours.

TEACHING A PAW TAP

PRECISE DESCRIPTION OF THE BEHAVIOUR

The dog will tap the palm of my hand. I choose this to be the left paw to right hand, or right paw to left hand, I teach this facing the dog. You can choose the opposite way around, as in right paw to right hand.

FUTURE OF THIS BEHAVIOUR

I want the dog to respond to anyone offering a low palm of hand

WHAT IS THE INITIAL ANTECEDENT

Trying to get the hidden food

WHAT WILL BE THE LONG TERM ANTECEDENT STIMULUS

Say hello and the offered palm

WHAT WILL BE MY REINFORCER TO BUILD THE STRENGTH OF THE BEHAVIOUR

Food treats

WHAT WILL BE THE LONGER TERM REINFORCER

Reaction from the recipient

Begin with the dog in the sit position, facing you, and sit on the floor with the dog. Place a treat in the palm of your hand and close it 80% of the way. The dog must be able to smell the treat and make some attempt to get their tongue between your fingers. Place the back of your hand to the floor in front of the leg associated with this hand.

Encourage the dog to sniff, by reinforcing the sniff with the piece of food—spring your hand open as they sniff. Once this has been successful 4 or 5 times, hold onto the piece of food for a bit longer, and reinforce extra hard investigation or even a paw helping the nose to success. Make success very,

very slightly harder each time by expecting extra effort, or the same effort for a longer period.

Repeat this about 20 times in one lesson and then take a break. On vary rare occasions a dog will not move onto tapping the fist with the paw, and in these circumstances use a small flower pot, or something that covers the food and allows for the scent to tease, and success comes from knocking the pot over with the paw to get the food.

Most dogs will try a paw when faced with a little frustration. Gain success in this about 50 times with each hand, and make sure the correct paw taps the correct hand. If they are insistent that only one paw works, check that the dog's weight is not too committed to the paw you want the dog to use. Lean slightly to the dog's left if you want the right paw to operate.

Once the presentation of your hand containing the food reliably gets success, mimic exactly the same gesture but this time keep the food ready to deliver in your other hand. Hold this other hand behind your back. As soon as the dog taps the empty hand, (which looks like it usually does when it contains the food), mark with a clicker or a "good", and then put the food into this fist hand to give to the dog.

It is important that the hand that gives the cue, the fist, also delivers the reinforcer or the dog will quickly discover to focus on the wrong hand.

Repeat this at least 20 times and then begin to gradually open the cue hand until it is an open palm. The dog should now have progressed from needing the hidden food as the antecedent to the hand gesture as the antecedent and the food only as the reinforcer.

Over the next 200 repetitions you will need to transit from sitting on the floor with the dog, to sitting in a chair, you not the dog, and then standing up but bending over, and then standing fully upright. For the small dog you will need to maintain some bend. Practice both hands equally and when reliable, and you are standing up, begin to introduce the verbal cue "say hello" just before you offer your hand.

If you want this behaviour to happen with many people in many different places it will take at least another 1000 repetitions with you in many different places, beginning with different locations around your own home, and then introducing familiar people who can mimic exactly your hand gesture.

This is a good example of something a dog chooses to do getting a positive response—food. The dog will learn more than just tapping your hand but also a lot about learning, experimenting and remembering what gets results.

But this is also a good example of poor management of error free learning. We may be lucky and get the tap we are looking for, but we may encourage a smack, all the claws extended for a scratch or a hesitant "wet" paw shake. With this example the only way to ensure these errors do not occur is not to pay for them, do not reinforce when scratched or whacked. Unfortunately this can leave a green dog without any information as to how to change their behaviour to one that will be successful. If you observe carefully you will begin to recognise the openings of an unpleasant contact—withdraw your hand quickly so that contact cannot be made, but still reinforce. This is attempting to split out the part that we like: moving your paw to touch, but removing the hand to prevent the bit we don't like.

If you have been through this struggle of trying to improve a behaviour closer to the desired result you will learn more than teaching a dog to paw tap, but also be motivated to look closer for error free learning situations.

TEACHING A PUP TO STAY UNDER CONTROL FOR GREETING

PRECISE DESCRIPTION OF THE BEHAVIOUR

Holding a position, either standing or sitting, to encourage and maintain during greeting. Control during a moderate level of arousal and anticipation.

FUTURE OF THIS BEHAVIOUR

A foundation behaviour for many control situations, greeting all visitors, and sometimes without direct reinforcement from the visitor.

WHAT IS THE INITIAL ANTECEDENT

In this case it is preventing jumping up through hand contact.

WHAT WILL BE THE LONG TERM ANTECEDENT STIMULUS

A person saying hello, direct eye contact and raised voices, back of hand being offered to be sniffed (where in the world did this originate?), people coming into the house, morning greeting, reunion after absence.

WHAT WILL BE MY REINFORCER TO BUILD THE STRENGTH OF THE BEHAVIOUR

Treats, lots and lots of treats, hand contact if calming and pleasurable to the pup.

WHAT WILL BE THE LONGER TERM REINFORCER

Food treats for people of medium to low value, (boring people). Attention for sixty seconds from beloved people. Treat from you for people that are definitely not doggy, or do not want to be touched.

The arousal is usually triggered by your arousal. The pup reflects your emotion and this arousal becomes reinforced with re-connection and attention. As it strengthens you can quickly build a nine month old dog that flies around the light fitting when you or visitors arrive.

Instead think constantly of prevention. As you begin to talk to the pup, do not get too excited or raise your voice, keep a calm body language and get your hands to the pup's height. If you ignore the pup they may experiment and jump at you to get to your hands or face.

If the pup is not wearing a collar place your hands on either side of their shoulders and fuss with your finger tips. If the pup does not desire physical contact, take treats down to the pup's level and deliver at a high rate, which means when one is finished offer the next one. It is better to offer 20 very small treats that can be quickly eaten than one that needs a full dinner service to enjoy, (although this can be a useful diversion if the visitors are demanding your attention).

If the pup is wearing a collar, drop one hand onto the collar tucking your thumb on the inside and use that very useful other hand to massage and fuss the pup. If you keep the collar hand locked at the elbow, any attempt at jumping should be unsuccessful and you should not receive a fat lip.

In public situations when the pup is on a lead, "Park" the pup, to prevent the innocent from facial injury.

TEACHING A YOUNGSTER WAIT UNDER CONTROL AT A DOORWAY

PRECISE DESCRIPTION OF THE BEHAVIOUR

When on lead on approach to the doorway the dog should come to a stop and check in with the owner, or when in the house or off lead, the dog should hold their position at the door until the door is open AND the dog is given the "go ahead" signal.

FUTURE OF THIS BEHAVIOUR

Life long request for a door to be opened, not demanded or assaulting the door. On arriving or leaving premises the dog is under control. The same principles can be transferred to getting in and out of the car, or crate.

WHAT IS THE INITIAL ANTECEDENT

Prevention and established behaviour of sitting, or standing, under control for food.

WHAT WILL BE THE LONG TERM ANTECEDENT STIMULUS

The door itself, and the cue of the hand raising to the door handle.

WHAT WILL BE MY REINFORCER TO BUILD THE STRENGTH OF THE BEHAVIOUR

Food treats.

WHAT WILL BE THE LONGER TERM REINFORCER.

Accompanying the owner through the door, especially powerful when variable strength, sometimes a walk, or playing in the garden.

This behaviour is ideal to teach young puppies that have yet to learn the pleasure of shooting through doorways to the treasures on the other side. Without that anticipation it is just a place. Take the youngster to the doorway and give a waft of the food treat available. Then cue the sit, with the pup facing the door opening. You can engineer this by having your back against the door, and the pup sitting in front facing you. Treat for the sit. Then transfer yourself to the pup's side, treat plenty of times in this position. Place your hand on the handle, if the pup remains sitting treat. If the pup gets up to go through the door (they already have experience of what is waiting the other side), remove your hand, wait 10 seconds and then cue the sit again, and treat if correct first time.

Next time you move to raise your hand to the handle only make half the gesture. If the pup break position, as above, if not then reinforce. On each subsequent gesture move closer to the handle without arousing the pup out of the sit position. Avoid warning them not to move, this is a great opportunity for the pup to teach themselves. What begins to happen is the gesture of going for the handle becomes a cue for a reinforcement.

Next lever or turn the handle without opening the door, and reinforce every couple of seconds for maintaining control. Open the door just an inch and again reinforce. If there is danger of the pup pushing the door to help themselves to reinforcement, keep one hand on the door. Work this through step by step until the door can be open and the pup remains in their control position. Avoid using the door to punish an attempt to go through, long term this will only be effective if you can shut the door.

The cue to proceed through the door will be to follow you. This may seem rather ridiculous when letting the dog into the garden on a cold and frosty morning, but those few inconveniences to ensure good manners "after you..." will last a lifetime.

If this door learning coincides with house training, which is most likely, either pick up the pup to take out for house training or ensure you get through the door way first and the pup follows.

If the dog has already learned to barge through doorways dragging you along, then see Chapter 6 on Re-Balancing Behaviour.

WALKING TOGETHER

PRECISE DESCRIPTION OF THE BEHAVIOUR

Many people refer to this as "loose lead walking", where in fact this is an outcome to measure the success of the behaviour you want to teach. The precise behaviour is "match your stride to mine and stay level with me". I see the dog as maintaining a location to my side bounded by a semicircle.

Reinforcement will be plentiful when the dog is within that semicircle. The skill the dog needs to acquire to concentrating on our pace and being able to match it.

FUTURE OF THIS BEHAVIOUR

Walking out at a pace comfortable for both of us, safe from traffic, or interfering with other road users. Being able to walk anywhere without anxiety about marking.

This is a fundamental understanding for the future of going for walks where the dog runs free, but returns to walk alongside me in times that require increased control.

WHAT IS THE INITIAL ANTECEDENT

This will be food reinforcement when in the semicircle.

WHAT WILL BE THE LONG TERM ANTECEDENT STIMULUS

The lead resting loose against the dog's shoulder and my speed.

WHAT WILL BE MY REINFORCER TO BUILD THE STRENGTH OF THE BEHAVIOUR

Food reinforcement when in the correct position.

WHAT WILL BE THE LONGER TERM REINFORCER

Going ahead together, long, safe walks in variety of places.

Begin with getting the pup accustomed to wear a collar and lead whilst you lure the dog to walk along with treats. This can begin in the house and graduate to the garden. Your luring should prevent the pup experiencing any yank on the collar from shooting off to investigate. The pups will be fed 3 times a day up to 5 months so this is an ideal time to use at least one meal a day for the reinforcement of learning life skills.

To familiarise the pup with the wide world try to carry the pup or sit in your parked car with the pup on your lap at a variety of places letting the pup observe life without needing to walk along as well.

The initial learning should reinforce the wearing of the lead and collar. No further experience should begin until wearing the lead and collar does not affect the pup, and they respond to your lure.

Graduate the luring to place the pup in a position by your side, be consistent to one side or the other during teaching. Toss the food behind the pup, and when they have eaten they will come forward into the perfect heel position. Again toss the food behind, if you are familiar with a clicker, click when the pup arrives in the right position. Teach this in a boring environment, your food reinforcer should not have to compete with any more interesting stimuli.

This will need batches of 20 repetitions in a variety of places, even if several of these are in the same location, you can begin to stand on a different spot. The pup should collect their treat as they race back to this lured position for the treat. Once this attitude and confidence is established as the pup runs to join you begin to stand up taking the treat higher, otherwise that life long back problem will resurface with a vengeance. Once comfortable and upright, begin to take a couple of steps forwards and treat when the pup maintains the area to your side. The lead is quite irrelevant for teaching this behaviour and should only be viewed as safety equipment that acts as in the long term as a cue.

At this point you can progress to teach formal competitive heelwork where the dog maintains focus on your hands or you can teach a more relaxed position where the dog observes their environment and maintains this position. The second option is the harder challenge since the pup will need to learn two behaviours simultaneously: maintaining position and observing the environment.

For the second option move into a more interesting environment, and let the pup be at your side, sitting or standing, observing the world around them. I often take, read: "carry", youngsters to our local tourist attraction and let them sit and watch the world pass by. This is littered with outdoor eating places and ideal for familiarisation. Every few 10–20 seconds lean down and deliver a treat if the pup is remaining at your side. If they move away lure them back to position and increase the treat rate. Find yourself in a win:win environment and ensure that your food treats are higher value than any surrounding temptations. The local dog class is NOT the place to teach this. The opportunity to communication with other puppies is likely to exceed your offerings, and pulling and frustration will begin.

People will want to say hello, some will want to take pictures, most will hopefully walk by. The pup needs to learn how to react to all types of interaction. Reinforce the pup for sitting still when someone walks by. This can be a major difficulty for some pups whose only experience with people is 100% attention and interaction. The people that want to greet should be given several treats to give to the pup for not pulling or jumping up. The relationship with your dog will last a lifetime—the people to practise greeting skills for about 3 minutes, work out for yourself your priorities, and do not let strangers screw up you pup's learning.

Now we have a pup who has a history of the Place By Your Side representing high reinforcement.

If at any time the environment overwhelms your food value, come to a stop, wait for the control to re-re-emerge and then reinforce. Most pups will try for that leaf, that frog, that child, but when there is no success they will come to a standstill. Under no circumstances follow the pup to the must-see feather, this will be the beginning of a life time of pulling. It is useful to begin teaching the Park (see below) at this stage so that you have a management tool for just being able to stand together without pulling.

It is advantageous to teach large dogs lead walking when the legs are still quite short. The pup will learn to trot along by your side and you will not need to break into a jog. As they grow taller you should have the "walk by me" concept well reinforced and they can manage their own stride.

Over the next few months you will need to be diligent that you do not succumb to the "just this once" occasion and let the pup pull you towards anything. Remember that Single Event Learning? If you can maintain your diligence until puberty arrives you are likely to have a dog for life that does not pull. During puberty much of this learning flies out the window and you will need to find a form of entertainment in many places whilst you Park the Dog and watch the ladies go by. Two steps, back into Park, three steps, back into Park. This is not the dog's fault, their brain is undergoing changes and demanding they respond to all things sexual, and all things ego orientated. Multi-tasking: walking with you, maintaining position and absorbing the Threats to Manhood, is beyond their capabilities. Avoidance is one solution!

Just remember that you must focus on the pup's learning at all times. Your early investment where every walk is a feeding opportunity will return with ease once the hormones have settled down.

PARKING

This is a life saving technique that can be used in hundreds of situations. If prevents many unwanted behaviours and allows you to relax with the dog safe and under control.

You will need a flat collar and lead at least 5' or 1.5m long.

Take the handle of the lead in the offside hand (the hand away from the dog). With the free hand take hold of the dog's collar at the back of their neck. Allow the lead to drop to the floor as if you were going to start skipping and stand on the lead.

For large and boisterous breeds this should be both feet, spaced apart to allow you to maintain balance. For the smaller breeds, or calmer dogs, one foot should be sufficient but make sure the lead is under the ball of your foot.

The length of lead must allow both you and the dog to remain standing comfortably.

Once in this position do not interact or reinforce the dog unless there is a health or safety issue.

Any jumping up will be inhibited by the lead, and there will be a stimulus of pressure on the back of the dog's neck from the collar. This is the long term cue for "I'm on a break". Then you can use your phone, watch the football, talk to a person, have drink. If you pay attention to the dog in the presence of this cue, you will make a life time of attention seeking behaviours.

This is our usual format in class for any time I wish to talk to the owners, or they want to watch a demonstration or take it in turns to practice a behaviour. After a very small amount of repetitions you can see the dogs recognise the pattern and naturally settle into a position comfortable to them. Some will stand, some will sleep, some will sit and lean on their owners.

I was invited to teach some foundation behaviours for a collection of 18 Gordon Setters and owners on a workshop. Gordons do not arrive with any concept of self control. The only element in this world that stimulates lack of motion is covered in feathers and is edible. We began the day with teaching the Park, and practicing it in many situations. Initially I walked up and behaved like a klutz to say hello to the lovely big doggy. Very aware the delicate nature of my facial bones. I only moved into the danger zone once the dog was securely parked. Lots of reinforcement and treats were delivered. Mostly the inexperienced dogs popped up and down on their parked leads, but I was safe. They also practiced standing reasonably near each other where the dogs could make gooey eyes at each other but not touch, and they practised the dogs remaining parked as another dog walked past.

This took most of the morning up to coffee time. As I took orders for refreshments these people were heading to their cars to settle the dogs and enjoy their well earned caffeine. Oh no, no, no. Dog goes out for a pee, time in the car is only if you need a pee. Everyone returned to the room, parked their dogs and I served coffee. This was a first. Cups of hot liquid and Gordons are not usually a recipe for relaxation.

By tea time not only were the people able to Park their dog and enjoy tea, but they also ate cake!

Be Seriously Impressed!

MAINTAINING BEHAVIOURS

Dogs work very hard at compromising their pleasures to our lifestyles and situations. They give up many of their doggy desires to share our lives and it is our share of the partnership to appreciate these small sacrifices. Regular appreciation, in dog values not your reinforcement of shopping for a new collar, will cement your relationship and make life with your dog a pleasant and fulfilling activity.

YOUR DOG'S SACRIFICES:

> Being stopped from reading the information left by the rabbit, fox, Labrador from down the road. I regard "good smells" as similar to old newspapers. I rear a litter of pups about once a year, in the house, and need copious amounts of newspaper for around a 6 week period. I do not have regular opportunity to read newspapers and beg from friends. I have been caught several times bending over to try to read a story through some puppy widdle. I was doubly frustrated when reading an interesting feature only to find the other half of the spread was… "unreadable". So imagine you have just seen the headlines to something interesting and whap! you get called off to hurry up or dragged forward on the lead. How irritating.

> You would really like to snooze in the sunshine, but for convenience and everyone else in the house the only comfortable place to sleep in is your bed, which is in the sunless utility room. Sigh.

> Visitors are arriving and you pick up the excitement of everyone, the frantic clearing up and cleaning—coo, someone important then. You can only share this excitement vicariously since you have been shut out to protect the furniture from your muddy feet, slobber and hair. All you want to do is join your pals…. sounds fun.

Reinforcement for the everyday behaviours that make your life easier, or the dog's more interesting need, to be variable. Once a month I obtain an ox heart from the butcher and roast this for great, No.1 treats. Far above the daily standard. Sometimes I take the juices from a roast and save them to fill toys with treats and dripping…. mmm yummy. On hot days I freeze pork belly strips as doggy lollipops. My everyday reinforcer will be some biscuit or dried treats, and the slightly above average is diced sausage or sandwich meats for regular training sessions.

BEHAVIOURS THAT DESERVE ATTENTION AND APPRECIATION:

Responding on the first call with a movement towards whatever you are indicating: go indoors, go outdoors, go into the kitchen, get off the sofa.

Responding to your name, but not barging through or creating a fuss if you are not included. Waiting you turn for training, dinner or treats.

Sitting under control for the lead to be clipped on.

Jumping into their cage in the van. Waiting in the van quietly when I arrive, not barging out of the cage gate.

Coming into the house instead of yapping at the gate. Job done!

Moving out of my way when I come downstairs with the laundry basket.

Settling quietly in the garden when I am working, watching TV, reading.

My reinforcement schedule will vary. On the days when I have the above average all behaviours will get paid, if nothing is to hand they will get a gentle touch, or scratch behind the ear depending on their preference. This variation between the highly valued treats and very-nice-thanks, maintains the behaviours stronger than the same reinforcer every time. But for the pup who is learning these behaviours, high reinforcement is always on offer.

Do not take good behaviour for granted. Once you have worked hard at re-balancing a behaviour you will begin to realise it is far, far easier to maintain what you want, rather than assume it will stay the same.

5 Reinforcement Patterns and Linked Behaviours

Dog training is more than just training a dog. It requires us to learn exceptionally good skills to keep up with the learning skills of the dogs. They survive without reference books, peer prompting, or note taking, but can remember that when you wear <u>that</u> jacket, you keep your treats in <u>that</u> pocket and moving your hand to those treats means you are going to collect a reinforcer. How long did they take to learn that—oh, maybe twice. To stay ahead of Single Event Learning you have to be really on your toes. When something happens that results in reinforcement it can be a lucky accident, and you hope the dog was not paying attention as to how they succeeded, but when it happens twice then you are in trouble—they were awake.

I was watching the dogs in the garden enjoying their bones and the youngest was well away from the others near the gate out of the garden. Tessie had finished hers and spied something beyond the gate that required a full vocal rush—probably the crows on the chicken feed bin. Well the youngster didn't wait around to see what she was going to do, but bolted under the hedge. "Well, hey …?", thinks Tessie, "His bone is now my bone". The very next meal time she took two seconds to look around the garden and repeat the successful tactic. Eating regimes have now been re-organised.

Think of that puppy you so adore and can't keep your hands off. He rushes up to you and enthusiastically jumps at you with joy. Your heart leaps at such a display of pleasure directed towards you that you find it difficult not to mirror the excitement. Ooops, no, must ask for a sit. Yay! A sit and mutual leaping begins. Double oops.

You have always believed that if you reinforce the wanted behaviours and ignore the unwanted behaviour that everything will turn out OK. The jumping at you with enthusiasm and joy will just fade away. Which planet do you live on? How did you think it was that easy? And two years down the road has the jumping with enthusiasm faded or is it well and truly fixed?

Firstly let's look at the "ignore the unwanted" principle. This is very effective at managing behaviours that are not going to receive any reinforcement. Ideal for anxious moments in young dogs. When they first spy a plastic bag flapping in the hedge, and start to become anxious, you should ignore the behaviour unless it progresses to a need for flight. By showing no reaction you clearly demonstrate to the youngster, who needs guidance and information, that this is not a serious threat and it doesn't bother you. By reacting to the pup, even in a "it's alright it won't bite" attitude, is a reaction, and reactions from people or other dogs can be reinforcers. You can inadvertently teach the dog to look for things to react to, to gain your attention.

I sit at the table eating my dinner, the pup comes over to seek attention. This is normally forthcoming, but this is the exception: when I am "sat up" with my arms actually on the table. He is completely ignored. Five minutes later I push back my chair, relax and this time he seeks attention he is successful. He will learn to discriminate the difference in my body language, and the attention seeking fades when not appropriate, and is reinforced when I am open to interaction. It may take more than a couple of attempts before his observation skill are acute, but all my adult dogs leave diners alone. I have ignored unwanted behaviours, *that received no other reinforcement.*

If the pup had dragged the table cloth as he sought attention and food landed on the floor as a result of this, you would be well within your rights to let loose an expletive, and just pray he did not make the connection between the behaviour and the jackpot. If that happened the cloth would be removed to avoid any experiments for a repetition, or eating would have been changed to a different location. Counter surfing is repeated because it is randomly successful. Don't leave food on the counters.

But if the pup jumped at you for attention when you are eating, you cued them to sit, and gave them some food, how did you expect that not to happen again? Just because on this occasion food is convenient, it is not a reason to reinforce the two behaviours—jumping up was reinforced by attention, and the sit was reinforced by the food. Guess what happens if the pup just sits? You don't notice. Then "just sitting" is unlikely to happen much more.

I was staying with some friends who have a delightful pug that has obviously been fed from the table..... by guests. The family were not mugged, just the guests. Yep, we dog lovers need to find a way to stop "friends" sabotaging our routines ... or perhaps that is their reinforcer? Have you noticed that when guests know you are interested in training they look for ways to get your dog to appear naughty?.... Hmmm. Anyway delightful pug starts making singsong snorts for attention, hitching up the volume every 10 seconds. Salad was on the menu, and a spare piece of onion found its way into my hand and offered to the pug-star. Hmm, single event learning, it went to bed. The next guest was given a severe mugging, but I was not pestered again. Onion was obviously not a reinforcer, it punished the behaviour in that environment with me, and was probably more powerful than simply ignoring (the noise was truly Pop Idol worthy), since her anticipation of something more tasty was pushed to the other extreme. Yes, I will give you attention, but it may not be of your choice.

The ignoring principle is only effective when there is no connection to the wanted behaviour. When the wanted behaviour originates from the unwanted the two become locked together.

wanted behaviour, showered with reinforcement

unwanted behaviour, ignored, no response

But...

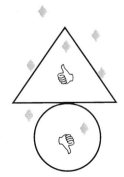

wanted behaviour, originates in unwanted behaviour, both become reinforced.

BEHAVIOUR CHAINS

Behaviours that happen directly one after the other can also be locked together. Such as: jump up for attention, cue "sit", sit gets reinforced. The whole chain becomes reinforced.

Either initiating the sit before jumping up was ignored, yes give yourself a mental slap, or the dog does not know how to sit without jumping up first. You can easily teach the dog to sit for treats, good boy. The more frequently this is practised the faster the sit will begin to become a highly reinforcing behaviour, since there is usually treats, dinner, walks, greeting etc, and the cue to sit can act as a secondary reinforcer, rather like a marker or a clicker. Whilst the dog is jumping at you, you cue "sit" (mark the jumping at you, why don't you) and link this into the reinforcing sit. A mark is a bridge—it connects behaviour to the reinforcer.

I see many of these chains of wrong behaviour right behaviour locked into a pattern. When a sequence begins to repeat itself you must look for the reinforcement, and separate the behaviours.

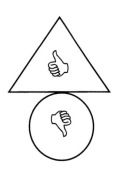

this combination get reinforced and paried together.

but can you be sure the dog knows how to do this alone?

YO-YO LEAD WALKING.

The dog walks forward to the end of the lead, you stop the walk, the dog returns to stand by your side, gets a treat. You set off and the smae pattern repeats.

One element of Yo-Yo walkers is an incompatible length between stride between dog and person. Kent and I can walk in perfect unison, our stride length matches, but his mother, Mabel, gets stuck between walking with me, which is slightly too slow for me, or trotting by my side, which is too fast for me. In her prime she would break between the two gaits, a few steps trotting then a couple of strides in walk, then a couple of steps trotting etc. This was a very jerky rhythm, but she always avoided pulling and demonstrated excellent understanding of having to walk at my speed—which is the essence of walking together. Now she is elderly I use a self retracting lead, which allows her several steps and then a stop to wait for me. An ideal piece of equipment for a dog that is already skilled at matching her stride to me, and stone deaf.

By reinforcing the position by your side AFTER the dog has gone out of position is building a pattern where reinforcement is only forthcoming when the dog come back to position, not for maintaining position.

AGGRESSING AND THEN GIVING ATTENTION.

This is a common chain commonly reinforced by the person's relief that the aggressing, or unwanted behaviour has stopped.

Your dog spies a dog in class, or on the street, that makes it apprehensive. Dogs are very good at sending threatening messages across a room. Your dog reacts, sparks up on all cylinders and shouts abuse at the offender. This gets a reaction from you "hush, don't be nasty" (read: stop embarrassing me). This reaction, which is emotionally charged from the embarrassment is read by the dog as support for reacting to the offender. You manage to interrupt the shouting and the dog pauses for a few seconds. Relief floods through you and you begin to feed copious amounts of food and reinforcing attention. This combination of behaviours quickly develops into a pattern.

I SAY AGAIN ...

Repeating a cue can become a pattern. It doesn't matter whether your dog is a highly tuned working partner or a pet, a cue is a cue, and if the second or third cue is the one that gets the reinforcer, then you are building a pattern which will soon become the norm. The dog hears cue number1, waits for cue number 2 (which is probably stronger pitched) and responds and gets a reinforcer. Tosh! And don't give me the excuse that you are lucky it happened at all. Your relief from getting some sort of result must not be the relevant reinforcer in this situation. "He didn't hear me first time", well he won't need to hear the first five times soon! By reinforcing the eventual result you are pairing the lack of any response, ignoring the cue, with the success of the response. This is a generic pattern that can easily transfer to all cues. If you require a dog to sit first time, no hesitation in a critical situation, then your cue to "get off", "down", "go to bed" must also only be reinforced when responded to the first cue. You cannot expect the dog to adjust to different standards on different occasions.

Avoiding repetition of cues is particularly important if the first response has not been the correct behaviour. If you take notes and observe what behaviour is offered instead, you may find a pattern building. Cue the "down" and the dog sits, cue the "down" again and the dog goes into the down, gets a treat. Ooops. You have reinforced a chain on the cue "down": sit, cue, down food. You have reinforced the incorrect response, you are building a pattern of error/correct behaviour.

CLOSE HEEL POSITION.

You are teaching the dog heelwork for competition. The dog drifts out of position, you cue "close", the dog moves in and gets reinforcement. If this is regularly repeated check that you have not built an error/correct pattern. This may have started because you stopped reinforcing the correct position and during one of those Single Event Learning episodes the dog discovered that if they drifted off your leg you woke up, cued close and they were given treats. How cool is that? There is also a high possibility that you can't walk in a straight line and you drifted off the dog instead.

SIMULTANEOUS BEHAVIOURS

Behaviours that happen simultaneously also get locked together when reinforced. In class we often teach a paw wave as an early behaviour for the clicker training class. This is taught in the sit position, since it is the mostly likely foundation that supports a paw action. When the paw movement is clicked and reinforced, so is the sit. Many months later, when the dog is cued to wave a paw, they will sit first, even without the cue to sit. The reinforcement was effective on the *whole* pattern of the behaviour, not just the isolated bit that we tend to see. This can be a useful strategy and many behaviours can be locked together. But when it happens unintentionally it becomes very hard to split the behaviour apart.

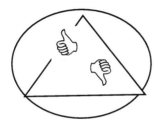

If you do not want the sit locked to the behaviour, or any other position, then during the learning or acquisition period, you must ensure that the rest of the body is inconsistently reinforced, ie: sometimes a sit, then a down, then a stand, then a lean etc.

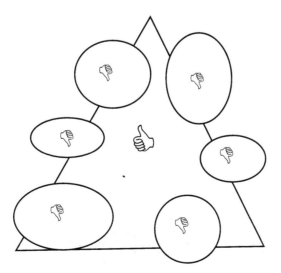

The wanted, correct behaviour is paired with variable, undesired behaviours.
The wanted behaviour becomes the common factor that is receives the most reinforcement.

COMMON BEHAVIOURS THAT LOCK TOGETHER:

Arousal and jumping at people

Arousal and barking

Walking to heel on a particular side

Sitting only in front of you

You can plan to lock collections of behaviours together, such as a controlled sit for putting on the lead and collar, a sit at a specific location for feed time. Success will depend on your consistency in requiring both behaviours to happen before reinforcement. "Just this once" you put the lead on when not sitting, and you will weaken the combined behaviour.

OOOOPS

When using reinforcement for learning, maintaining and re-balancing behaviours there will be occasions when the dog makes an error. I can guarantee that you will be superior at making errors than the dog, but the dog will sometimes forget, sometimes be day dreaming, sometimes see a threat or opportunity that you haven't noticed and not be able to comply with your wishes.

How you handle this situation is vitally important. You need to be able to communicate that the behaviour offered was not worthy of a reinforcer, but that the dog is not punished, just the behaviour. If this is done ineffectively the dog will give up trying to find the correct behaviour. If you need to repeat this "oops" twice in a row, then you have taken it one step too far. Reconstruct the learning to build the dog's confidence, not destroy it. This may only take an extra 60 seconds but be invaluable in the dog's self esteem.

"Oops" is just a response that indicates no luck this time, let's try again? It is only effective in a situation where a reinforcer is on offer, and the dog expects a reinforcer, AND the behaviour has been well constructed, practised and fluent. It should never be used to teach behaviour, it only indicates what should NOT be done, it cannot indicate what is desired. It should serve to trigger a re-think, and leaves eagerness for a repetition: "Oh, can I try again?" Never: "I have no earthly idea what you what or what that is supposed to mean."

When the dog is expecting information in the form of a reinforcement, with or without a bridge, silence and lack of response will have the effect of punishment. When free-shaping a new behaviour there appears to be continuous silence, but we let the reinforcers do the work, whilst we observe. Trying to puzzle out what is required to get a reinforcer can be quite exciting, but dogs have different tolerant levels of how long they will puzzle before they give up. We build youngsters keen on puzzle solving by making the early puzzles easy, and only increase the difficulty without them noticing, a sure indication of their increasing skills. In these situations our body language "talks" to the dog, reacting every few seconds with reinforcement, or focussing on their learning.

Once this behaviour is established we can get over keen to jump to the final stage. The dog doesn't respond to the cue as expected, and is met with silence. What does that mean? I don't only use "oops" but I usually add "no bananas this time" and fall on the floor laughing.

The timing of "oops" is also important, you cannot stare at the dog with raised eyebrows in expectation and after five seconds realise that they aren't going to do it and then give the "oops". When the dog is cued to "down" and is successful, then a response that it is it correct will happen within microseconds. It may not be the delivery of reinforcement but a marker, or an expression, or a cue for another behaviour. Five seconds of silence communicates what? Even if the dog responded by trying something else (which tells me a lot about your training style), do you want to reinforce the eventual correct behaviour? Are you not building a pattern or teaching the dog to cycle through everything they know until you are happy?

As soon as the "oops" is delivered, clear the air, re-set the dog to try again. If the next attempt is another error you must re-set and go back to the re-building to refresh the dog's understanding.

Clear information is reinforcing. It removes confusion, uncertainty and the burden to try and understand us from the dog.

UNLOCKING PATTERNS

I sometimes think it would be a good investment to have a camera follow you for a day through all your contact with your dog. Often we do not recognise errors when we are wrapped in the centre of them, and can only see what is happening by externally viewing the protocols through different eyes. The camera is rather harsh at revealing the body language that we don't appreciate at the time.

But if you have now realised that you have patterns of error correction in your routines, those three calls from the garden to get the dog in late at night, congratulate yourself—you are seeing through new eyes. That is the first step, and the hardest one, since I have faith that not only will you break the habit but begin to see it more often and avoid starting a new pattern.

You may need to re-balance the behaviours and remove the reinforcers to get the unwanted paired behaviour to disappear, but generally try to stop the connection between the two. This is very effective in the early stages of the pattern establishing, but not after several repetitions, the removal of reinforcement can effectively push the pair together stronger in an extinction burst. This is the effect of something you have come to expect to happen, over a long reinforcement history which suddenly fails to happen. Your first reaction will often be of forgiveness, let's just try again. But if you do not understand why there is no longer reinforcement you will try harder to get a response. The key to this technique is the lack of understanding. If I go to switch on the light and do not get illumination, I will not try to switch the light harder, or faster to get it to work. I understand that either the bulb has gone, or that the electricity supply has failed. I understand zip about petrol mowers, and if the machine fails to start first time I will certainly get my strength girded up to try harder and harder. Somewhere in the past, several "hard" attempts were probably successful. I suspect the first few attempts may need to "warm up" the bits that do their stuff, but that doesn't trigger a calm approach to grass cutting.

When the pup jumps up for attention I don't immediately react with reinforcement for the offered sit, although I take note that there was some self correction in process. The pup jumps up, and then tries a sit, I may walk away, talk to another dog, but keep the pup in vision, after few seconds of jump free actions I will cue sit or just give attention for the absence of jumping. I appreciate it is hard to ignore that delicious moment when they correct themselves. On the first occasion you will reinforce, and probably the second or third, but if you find yourself reinforcing it regularly then you are in trouble. The pattern has become established.

Always seek prevention, error free association as a strategy, make sure the pup cannot error in the first place—be awake, be on your toes and be what your learner needs you to be.

6 Re-Balancing Behaviours

For every situation where there is an unwanted behaviour there is an alternative, acceptable, behaviour. Your first, and most important task, is to clearly identify what this behaviour is. I often need to remind clients that they don't want to "stop their dog barking" but actually be able to say: "thanks, job done". Dogs bark, it is what they were designed to do to communicate. If they don't get communication they will continue the behaviour.

Tessie enjoys an Evening Choral, very likely something has passed by the garden in the neighbouring woods that Should Not Be There. A fox, a badger, a hedgehog. Left to her own devices the barking can prolong for 15–20 minutes (I was on the phone!). My collies wouldn't stir for passing wildlife and show no reaction to her call to arms. Mabel is stone deaf and doesn't respond, and her father is comfortably tucked up and is old enough to assess the choices available: comfort or supporting the noisy child in the garden? Hah, no contest.

In consequence I am the only one going to listen to her, which is stimulated by a small degree of irritation from the necessity that I now need to give up my comfort, change out of the warm slippers, put on a coat and trudge to the bottom of the garden. I arrive to her listening post, she tells me what has been going on, I tell her thanks very much, I appreciate her alertness and readiness to defend, but the job is now completed, I have noticed, and now we'll go back in to watch the rest of the film, of which I have probably missed the best bit. No wonder one could be tempted to stand at the door and shout. Shouting at a barking dog serves very little purpose, the dog will either:

See it as back up support (reinforcing through mirrored behaviour)

A distance wail, "come into the house, I have your favourite biscuit" and read: she doesn't want to go out into the cold, but will try to bribe me to come in, and if I keep barking for longer the offered bribe may increase. I feel lucky tonight.

Other options may be regularly tried, like the buckets of water or thrown "interrupters" but the dog may see that as a challenge to their Watch Dog skills, and return to duty with more intensity.

Ignoring communication, waiting for the unwanted behaviour to fade, can be a long evening's noise, irritating more than just you, but all your neighbours as well. The dog may view a "no reaction" as a need to continue the warning, since the threat is still present, and you maybe unable to hear them (TV turned up too loud). The barking will only fade when the threat is passed AND the dog's arousal level has returned to normal. In their aroused state of the first need to Alarm, every small trigger is magnified. You must be able to recall that night time feeling of hearing an out of place sound, and then every sound after that makes you twitch?

Ideally, we listen, tell the dog we have "heard them", job done, and now let's return to the house. As the dog accompanies me to the house, I will reinforce with attention and treats. I do not treat the cessation of barking, which would open up the danger of making an error correction pattern, but the next behaviour: accompanying me to the house. After an amazingly short number of repetitions, I am able to keep my slippers on and call her alarm barking to the house for reinforcement. I don't think I would have much success in preventing the barking since the stimulus are wide and varied and out of my control, but I can reduce the duration of the alarm. This strategy is only successful in the mild to medium threat alarm. If it is a serious alert, someone in trying to break down the fence, then I would not expect, or desire, success— keep on going poppet.

To be able to rebalance any behaviour you will need to be in a position to remove the reinforcer from the unwanted behaviour.

PAVEMENT SWIMMING VS WALKING TOGETHER

Pulling on the lead was taught by you. You followed the pup, you followed the dog when it was easier because you were in a hurry to go out. You reinforced this behaviour. Ethically you cannot punish the dog with the use of aversive equipment to cover for your own laziness or ignorance. I know that is not your choice since you are reading this book and looking for a non-aversive solution. You can use preventative equipment, such as a head collar/harness, but this will not teach the dog not to pull.

By recognising that your behaviour reinforces the pulling you cannot re-balance this to a relaxed arm situation without changing your behaviour. From the dog's view it is easier to understand this removal of reinforcement with a lead that is at least 5 foot long, on a non-aversive collar. That means no check chains or other painful neck wear. They find it easier with a clear location, at 5 foot, that is no longer reinforced, and the clear location, at my side, which is reinforced. Short leads muddy this delineation making it harder for the dog to work out what is desired.

Firstly the dog will need to learn how to walk at your pace. See the section on preventing pulling page 79. If the dog is beyond attraction to treats, then you will need to stop and stand still to stop the behaviour. Often dogs become so highly aroused when out for a walk, anticipating arriving at the park, or sniffing and browsing the road side, that treats may not be an option.

Make sure you hold the lead in such a way that when the dog pulls, your arms do not move, neither do you step forward or jerk backwards. Arm waving behind a pulling dog is very rein-forcing, encourage a continuation of the behaviour. I advise clients to place the handle of the lead over their off-side wrist and hold the lead with that hand. Then place the other hand about half way down the lead to support the slack. Make a loop to hold the lead with both hands at waist height. The length between the hands and the dog should be short enough to prevent the dog tripping on the lead if at your side, but not so short that the dog will always be on a tight lead even when in the right place and walking at your speed.

Firstly just stand still with your feet slightly apart. If the dog tries to pull there will be no reaction from you, you must "make like a tree", actually more like a branch-less concrete post. If the dog is tied to an immovable pillar visualise the reaction, they will try to get the pillar to move maybe once or twice and then recognise that the behaviour is going to be unsuccessful, and stop

pulling. Extreme situations of over arousal through excitement or fear may trigger pulling, but we would not be aiming to teach in those situations just yet. If you feel the dog may succeed in moving you, hitch the dog up to the pillar with a back-up lead, and stand by the dog as if you were the concrete pillar. Associate the lack of success from concrete with your determination to not continue to reinforce this behaviour. It may surprise you to learn that the dog quickly analyses their chances of success with a "tester" pull. They assesses whether you are awake or day dreaming, and if this is another person with a less stringent set of boundaries. Even my "never-pull-unless-it's-an-emergency" Kent, will test his walker very subtly and begin pulling in less than 60 seconds.

The first step has to be removing reinforcement through your movement. The dog spies a post to sniff, pulls over to it and you follow, you have reinforced the behaviour with a double joy—getting to the smell, *and* dragging you off your path.

Once you can stand still and have a pull-free moment, count to five and then reinforce. You can choose a variety of options depending on what would be reinforcing to the dog at that moment. You may touch them, smile and talk, or deliver a treat, or you can take a step forward. For the dog that is focussed on getting to a specific location taking one step towards that location IS the reinforcer. For the dog that has no idea where we are going, re-connection, some conversation is the reinforcer. For dogs learning to accompany you, treats or a touch would be spot on.

The walk can only progress, one step at a time, if you can return at any time to the reinforce-less standing still, making like a pillar. If the dog is over aroused, a more appropriate reinforcer of connection, touch or food, is first choice since the one step forward can act as the "release" and the dog sprints out of the starting blocks. The dog needs to be relaxed standing at your side before forward progress. For the highly excited, the protocol is one step forward progress and stop for relaxation and control, one step, stop etc. Continual forward progress for the over excited can build up such as level of stimulation that no learning will happen. Teaching these dogs self control on lead, and walking together cannot be time restrained. The first lesson may take you 30 minutes to progress through the front door to the kerbside, but each lesson, well taught, is money in the bank and will pay dividends as you progress steadily. If the dog pulls out of the front door, how can you expect them not to pull going down the road or to the car?

Make sure you have taught the dog "Parking" which teaches the dog about a resistant-less lead, where pulling has no outcome and it is a lot easier on your arms and back if you have a big dog. (Page 82)

The strategy will be small slow steps, slow enough that the dog does not build up to a trot, and maintains a relaxed, controlled awareness of being at your side and moving in concert with you. Expect the dog to revert to the unwanted behaviour. The number of times depends on how long the dog has been reinforced for being a puller, and the arousal of the situation. Teaching this is more effective on boring places like post free (no opportunities for boys to mark), critter-less, empty car parks.

You will be able to use forward progress as a reinforcer. The behaviour of relaxing under control at your side when standing still is reinforced by connected progress forward, at a slow controlled pace. The more the dog wants to proceed the sooner they will learn to control their pace to get where they want.

Over time you will be able to build up through increasingly difficult criteria. Beginning with the slow stroll with your arms at your waist, to the slow stroll with your arms relaxed at your side, and then moving the pace upward to trotting, if that is comfortable for you. At any time you see the dog moving forward to a pulling position, you must take your arms back to your waist, and stand still.

Do not fall into the temptation of reinforcing the "oops" self correction of the dog. The dog goes forward, you stop, they go "oops" and return to your side, you step off again. This is building the Yo-yo dog of forward, stop, backwards. Always insert that five second pause, after the dog has self corrected and is standing at your side. Be prepared to set a criteria higher than five seconds if you notice the Yo-yo starting, add in a sit for 20 seconds as well. This will be reinforced by progressing with the walk, NOT the self correction. If self correction is reinforced then it is logical that the dog must error in the first place to be able to self correct.

ENJOYING PLAYING WITH FRIENDS VS THAT'LL DO, HOME TIME

This is just one example of a recall to you when the something else is on offer that far exceeds what you have to offer.

Initially I want you to assess whether the dog has a really good understand and response to being called. Mabel had a wonderful habit of turning to face me when I called her "Yes, that's my name... and.... ?" She trained me to be

I was interested to hear a great analogy born of the advent of word processors. All of us have tricky words that cause us to repeat the same spelling errors. If each time you back space to delete the error and re-correct it then you are not learning to type the word correctly in the first place. You should delete the WHOLE word and retype it correctly before you progress, otherwise you will never learn to not make this mistake.

This technique will not produce 100% error free text, but it has improved my keyboard skills enormously. I did need to slow down to maintain accuracy but in the long term this improved my speed since I spent less time re-correcting.

perfectly clear what was expected of her, since without that communication she quickly returned to what she was doing.

Does you dog always respond around the house is you call from one room to another?

Does your dog always respond when you call them in from the garden?

"Always respond" is defined as Now, not: "in a minute when I've finished what I'm doing". Sure, they need to complete their toilet, but you can see that they are focussed on the next activity: coming towards you. They do not have time to complete reading that interesting article, digging the hole or yapping at the birds.

"Coming to you" is defined as a reasonable pace with focus on where they are going, no allowance for window shopping on the way.

If you cannot answer yes with certainty to these expectations you must first ensure a very strong, and long reinforcement history on simple recalls from average situations BEFORE the dog is allowed to learn that if they ignore you, you cannot do anything about it. Ooops.

To smarten up the domestic recall, around the house or garden, make sure you only call once, but with clear volume and information as to what you want. We begin this in puppy class by teaching the pup to take food from the palm of the hand, one treat at a time. Once the pup is really interested in this game, you can divide their dinner into small bites and use it as well, we add on an association with their name "called" and a cue of your choice: "Here", or "Come", or "Me". This pairing needs to be strong and life long. If your pup arrives a few times and finds an empty hand, staying outdoors, or sleeping in the sunshine will have more appeal than an empty hand and a tickle on the head. A recall is very often a counter instinctive behaviour, ie; returning to you when something far more interesting is happening is second choice. If Pavlov's dog were not fed after the bell was rung for how long do you think they would produce saliva when they heard a bell? Association conditioning begins to fade very rapidly, and in the case of recall training, the alternative behaviour begins to increase in appeal equally rapidly, extinguishing your recall to hand.

Every day I feed my dogs, at every meal, I repeat the association of Name & Here. You feed your dogs every day, spending the energy on remembering to pair the cues is no hardship. This pairing must be viewed as life long. You need to build a reflex type of response, not a ponder and the dog making a choice between a sit at the front gate watching the people go by or a dry biscuit? Hmm... tricky.

Begin with this pairing, and implant it as much as possible throughout the day. Keep a bowl of treats by your kettle or coffee machine, and every time this goes into production, go into training. (Soon your dog will learn to arrive as they hear the kettle fill up!)

If the dog does not respond, under no circumstances repeat yourself. You may want to be forgiving and excuse them because they weren't listening, but make sure your call is of adequate volume that "not listening" is only an excuse, not a reason. If you get no response, you must go to the dog, give them a reminder of the reinforcement on offer, a whiff of the treat on the nostrils, and then return to the place you called. If you still get no response then what ever the dog is doing is more reinforcing that the food you have on offer. Up your reinforcer, show them the ball, toy, promise of a game etc.

We are often asked in class whether the owners will "always need to use treats". Yep. If you want to keep this essential management tool in good working order reinforcement will ALWAYS be needed. But as you are now seeing life through the eyes of opportunity use the occasions that the dog finds reinforcing as training for recalls, training for control, training for connection. If your dog loves to jump into the car, recall from the garden to the car. "Mabel, Here, In the car". If your dog enjoys running upstairs in the morning, jumping on the sofa to sit by you, coming in for their dinner, these are all opportunities to associate coming to you for a reinforcer. Mine all loved to be groomed. The box of necessities comes out to the table and the dog race around in excitement, I call on one dog to jump up and have the opportunity to practise a call away from great and exciting play, which is probably my greatest competitor in the reinforcement stakes.

Once you have the domestic recalls at the best standard they can be, begin to increase the difficulty of leaving whatever it is to return to you. But, you must be in a situation where you can get to the dog to remind them of the reinforcer. Recalls from a couple of arm's length away can be stimulated by the smell of your offered food, but over a distance the dog may not see the hand or smell the treat. If you want reliable response from the garden, take the dinner to the garden, split into 10 portions and practise around the garden. The reinforcement history must parallel the environment. If the dog only learns this behaviour in the house, then in the house is the only place where it is reliable.

In new areas, if necessary, put the dog on a light line. You will not use this to pull the dog towards you, but walk down the line to prevent the dog from moving away. If they began to return towards you the line would be irrelevant. Lines need to be planned with some thought. You can choose a weight between kite-line to washing line. The heavier the line the more the dog will associate the need to recall with the line, ie. they will only recall when on the line, but have discovered that when not on the line (that dratted Single Event Learning again) you will just stand by helplessly and they can carry on with their own shopping. Lines will get tangled in the undergrowth and around the legs of an exuberant dog. Try to let the line "drag" as opposed to carry it, and only stand on it when your call has not been responded to.

Gradually begin to increase the reinforcement value of the "shop windows": perhaps another family member is playing with the dog in another room. You call from the kitchen, they will stop playing with the dog and come to you for a treat, and as a bonus reinforcer you can send them back to play. You are out on a walk, with your dog on lead, and meet up with their best play mate. Before they get to run free, you let them begin to play on lead, recall your dog from this high reinforcer, treat or give great attention and then let them return to play, when you are ready, as the Bonus Reinforcer.

If you get into a no response situation, NEVER inform your dog of your helplessness, do not repeat the recall. You can try the strategy of "go hunting", which means you need to find a squirrel to chase, and rabbit hole to poke around or birds to shoo off the ground. Returning to you then is an instinctive behaviour: co-operative hunting, and more likely to interrupt the window shopping.

Do not take this behaviour for granted. It can be easily established with young pups since they are usually hungry, usually regard you as the source of most reinforcement and will eagerly comply. As they grow with experience and changing hormones their priorities of "window shopping" will begin to increase and establish. Remember a recall is always to touch your hand (so that you can capture) and is not a pass by when you change direction, I use a "this way" to indicate the hunt is moving onto new ground.

INSTINCTIVE RE-BALANCING

Nearly all behaviours in need of re-balancing are the contest between an instinctive behaviour that is self reinforcing and management to prevent that behaviour. If we don't have neighbours, barking at the bottom of the garden is not a problem, if we didn't have traffic, a recall in the park is not a necessity. If we never met other dogs or people a recall off play or greeting is redundant.

Re-balancing is often the contest between dogs behaving as dogs, and modern societies requirements and expectations of co-operative living. We MUST continually reinforce to maintain counter instinctive behaviours, if you begin to go easy on this the instinctive behaviour will begin to emerge, and each time it is exercised it will grow in strength making is harder and harder to re-balance.

Teach the wanted behaviours when the dogs are young, build a strong and long reinforcement history, and ensure the unwanted behaviours never get a toe hold.

Through the book I refer to some of my dogs and have included their profiles so that you can get to know them.

MABEL

12 Years old. The undisputed Queen.

A clicker child who proved the flexibility of its application. Taught me that I can be managed by her expressions, frustration and entertaining habits.

KENT

8 Years old, son of Mabel, although he doesn't seem to remember it.

Typical large, all male, Gordon. Tried to learn lots of things but has only ever enjoyed running, looking for birds, eating, sleeping and sex.

TESSIE

6 Years old, daughter of Kent. Came to live with me at four years old.

Was in a single dog household, quite highly strung, with obsessive behaviours. Always fun, makes me laugh and thinks collies are great toys.

QUIZ

10 years old, with her grandson Time.

A clicker child who taught me diligence, accuracy and to learn what I clicked is exactly what I got. A great mother and grand-mother, indulgent in the right amount, tolerance in balance and everyone's pivot.

Time is the ninth generation of my collies.

SPECK

4 year old collie, lives for action, takes his jacket off to work—sheep would be nice, but bats, birds and his sister will substitute. *(centre)*

FLINK

2 year old daughter of Speck and Quiz. A great young mum, but would rather push her sleeves up and be working. *(right)*

QUICK

1 year old son of Speck and Quiz. Very much son of his father, Kent's favourite companion. Who know why, but they always greet with great passion.

DOT

Sibling to Speck. Enjoys running circular patterns to irritate Speck, and always needs something between the teeth... grass, pegs, shoe laces, leaves...